the spark

Why Passionate Young Social Entrepreneurs Are Working To Change The World

Dedication

With appreciation to **Dr. Mike Kami**, **Ken Langone** and **Doug Curling.** Their faith, support, encouragement and wise counsel provided the energy not only to rekindle the spark within me, but also to ignite it into an enduring flame.

Contents

Foreword

"We need renais

in a technology-

a human sance

driven world."

Our world has changed. Transformation swirls all around us. We sense this in our communities, schools and places of worship. We feel it viscerally in our family interactions, personal relationships and workplace environment—certainly in public behavior and political discourse. Unease, uncertainty, dislocation, the sense that things are somehow slipping from our grasp are its hallmarks. Yet, change is as constant as it is unsettling. Five hundred years before Christ, the Greeks worried that onrushing change would herald the decline of their civilization. Correctly, as it turned out.

The exponential change we've experienced in the last decades is unique in history. It has not been driven by the age-old and very human lust for power, land, treasure, conquest or dominance, nor by the clash of civilizations or deep-rooted enmity. In fact, no human impulse is triggering this transformation. Technology, specifically information technology—the magic that enables our smart phones, tablets and Internet access—has advanced so far and so fast that our mortal brains cannot keep pace with our own creation. It's as if time itself has accelerated, and the borders of our lives are being compressed and diminished.

Technology is not Frankenstein's monster. Along with millions of others, I made a very good living as a technologist. Throughout history, technology has supported, enabled and empowered practically every social and scientific advance. Of itself, technology is neither good nor bad; it reflects whatever hand is on the trigger. We live surrounded by wonders unimagined in the 20th century but also by the reality of Internet predation, bullying, criminality, abuse and mindlessness that haunts all of us. But more disturbingly, it targets our children.

Our deep-seated fear that the human hand and the human heart will slip from technology's trigger (a familiar theme in sci-fi films and novels) is proving true. In fact, at times, there may be no hand on the trigger. Technology is racing away from us; not sentient but mindless, like the animated broomsticks that nearly drown Mickey Mouse in the *Sorcerer's Apprentice*.

There is no sorcerer with magic powers to assist us. Yet, our destiny doesn't have to unfold this way. We need to reassert our humanity, with all its grace and wonder, beneath our technology. We need to strengthen this vital connection and begin to transform today's chaotic world. To accomplish this, we must look to our own hearts to the goodness and kindness within all of us and create a human renaissance in a technology-driven society. And then journey to engage the world.

The pioneers in this journey are our youth. Among them, a new generation of "social entrepreneurs" is working quietly and selflessly for the greater good.

These young people are the heart and soul of this renaissance. Like all pioneers, they cannot survive on their own. They need help and support from families, mentors, teachers and the broader community in which they live, and also from individuals with passion, means and vision to understand the importance of these young men and women.

I cofounded GivingPoint to support and encourage youth's passion to create a better tomorrow. But how do we really help them change their communities and the world? It's simple. Imagine passengers boarding an endless train on a magnificent journey, embarking one person at a time, each young man and woman reaching out to help the next traveler onboard. I invite you to join this journey, to use our knowledge and insight to help power the human renaissance. Feel free to travel other paths or routes to assist this transformation. Selflessness and service to others can take many forms. I promise you a grand adventure that will transform our world in ways you can hardly imagine. There is a seat reserved for you. All aboard? The train is leaving the station!

—**Derek V. Smith**

Part

1

The Spark

Chapter

1

Change

"Technology requires a human hand on the trigger. And a human heart to guide it."

—Derek V. Smith

I've stepped away from the corporate world. Blessed with financial security, a loving family, friends, good health and well-being, all the trappings of the American Dream, I was successful, yet, unfulfilled. A spark swirled deep within me. I'd carried it from childhood, a desire to do something more with my life, to find a cause that would harness the knowledge, skills and lessons I'd acquired for the greater good and make a difference in the lives of others. Such passion exists in every human heart, waiting to be recognized and set free. Sometimes the spark flickers or dies. Often it lies dormant. In my case, it was my father, Dr. Donald L. Smith, a college professor who counseled me to pursue something larger than self-interest and to never define success solely in economic terms. The Civil Rights and Native American movements were his great passions. My personal journey was far less tumultuous, centered in the world of business and commerce—until a terrible day in the fall of 2001 when I stood in the ruins of the World Trade Center. Soon after, I would visit a room filled with thousands of orange-capped test tubes containing bone fragments of World Trade Center victims. Our company's forensic laboratory had been tasked with extracting DNA samples from which identification would be attempted. I knew several of the victims personally.

The world had changed. I'd changed. My career had carried me to technology's leading edge. I'd witnessed the digital world come into being with all its blessings. Yet, something vital was missing. It struck me that technology, for all its transformative power, also was becoming an instrument to dehumanize. Huge swaths of the Internet were the domain of predators pumping filth, violence and dysfunction into society. Selfishness and greed were, consciously or unconsciously, being portrayed in popular culture as a new norm. The evidence was everywhere, the consequences unthinkable, beyond even the perversion of turning airliners into weapons of mass destruction. It was a threat to the very virtues—selflessness, tolerance, generosity and idealism—that make us human. It was a menace directed at the young people who will inherit the world.

My friend and colleague, Doug Curling, and I believe that youthful idealism, passion, selflessness and commitment are linked directly to self-esteem, satisfaction and future success. We became convinced that engendering and supporting these values among young people would set the stage for a new human renaissance. We decided to pool our time and resources to test our convictions. Kids, immersed in all the tumult, strivings, aspirations and disappointments of youth, would be our proving grounds. We chose Gen Z. They are today's teenagers who are being buffeted by overwhelming technological change and who cling to their cell phones and tablets the way Doug and I cherished vinyl records and footballs. We saw a generation of uncertain, uncommitted, but well-meaning youngsters trying to figure out who they are and what their place will be in the world.

We created a 501(c)3 charitable organization to support our would-be "social entrepreneurs." We named it GivingPoint. Our approach was to avoid the perceived free-labor model many nonprofit organizations use when assigning youth volunteers to projects and causes. We would encourage young people to get involved in real-world issues and concerns (e.g., homelessness, aging, environment, education) that mattered to them personally. In effect, it would be an organization to give them permission to pursue their passions, providing the resources (e.g., human, technological and financial) needed to achieve their goals.

GivingPoint leverages the simple imperative that high school students must perform a specified number of community service hours to satisfy their diploma requirements. Given our technology background, we created a social platform (mygivingpoint.org) that allowed students to find, fuel, and pursue their unique civic passions. It allowed them to track and verify their service hours. We engaged hundreds of nonprofit organizations (e.g., Habitat for Humanity, YMCA, the Humane Society) in need of volunteers. Later, we would build in networking, blogging, educational and other capabilities. In essence, it was a structured support system for young social entrepreneurs. We assumed, incorrectly as it turned out, that equipping young people primarily with technological and financial resources that it would allow them to move forward, unfettered, in pursuing their passions.

It didn't happen.

We soon realized that technology requires not only a human hand on the trigger but also a human heart to guide it. Our "secret sauce" became not a multimillion-dollar technology platform, but a companion cadre of caring, willing and experienced mentors who guided our volunteers forward. Together, they created a new "social philanthropy," no less valuable than the millions of dollars provided by philanthropists and foundations.

GivingPoint, designed as both a call to action and a new approach to philanthropy, is supported, as you will see, by some of our country's great businesses and philanthropists. Every time a GivingPoint member connects with a senior citizen in a nursing home or reaches out to a lonely latchkey kid, the impact grows larger and more influential. Over time, we believe such passion will ultimately create a better, more connected and responsible world.

Within months of inception, GivingPoint enrolled more than 2,000 students. That figure now approaches 13,000, constrained only by a controlled growth plan and necessary financial and mentoring resources. GivingPoint's impact is more profound than our spiking numbers and positive community buzz. We've proved that despite the distractions, pressures, and sometimes chaotic circumstances of young lives, the teens who rallied to us wanted and needed to be involved in meaningful things. Many

We created a 501(c)3 charitable organization to support our would-be "social entrepreneurs." We named it GivingPoint.

so-called and mislabeled "ordinary" kids are proving themselves extraordinary, vast reservoirs of passion and commitment are now being tapped for the greater good. Ultimately, when asked what they are really passionate about, they collectively answer, "Something greater than ourselves."

To support the most dedicated and committed of these youth, we took a further step, creating the GivingPoint Institute (GPI). With significant financial support from philanthropist Bernie Marcus, a founder of The Home Depot, GivingPoint provides leadership training and instruction for a small, self-selected group of young people whose desire, commitment and concern for others demands nourishing. We engaged a number of highly skilled volunteers from leading companies such as Oracle, The Coca-Cola Company, Goldman, Sachs & Co., GolinHarris, Georgia Tech and Keller Williams Realty to conduct workshops and seminars. Our youngsters receive real-world, hands-on instruction and support in budgeting, planning, fundraising, marketing and public relations. It is an investment, as you will see, that is already paying dramatic dividends.

Grace, one GivingPoint Institute member, immediately put these lessons to work building a curriculum that teaches preschool children about volunteerism. Personally, she cares about helping sick children, feeding hungry children and caring for animals. But like her name, Grace's aspirations soar much higher. "I want to build a new generation of teens and young adults," she says, "who have such a passion for service it becomes second nature to them." She imagines a world where giving of oneself is as spontaneous an impulse as sending a text.

Of course, GivingPoint is not the magic bullet that will reverse all the consequences of living in a risky, uncertain and rapidly changing world. Nor will it reach all the isolated young people simmering with frustration and disappointment, or instantly enlighten their self-involved peers or disengaged parents. But for many, it is proving to be life-changing.

It is still a work in progress. Much like the startups Doug and I were involved in during our corporate careers, it has lots of what-ifs to be answered and fine-tuning to be done. Like our adolescents, GivingPoint needs nurturing, support and partners. Our intent is to share our vision and our technology freely with other community-based youth development leaders and organizations around the country so that the spark we've kindled becomes an enduring flame.

No youth with the desire to serve a cause greater than self-interest should ever feel alone or powerless. Not ever. GivingPoint underscores an indisputable truth: a cohort of young men and women are willing to answer the call of their better natures. You're about to meet a few of them. And they are just the beginning.

Part II

The Social Entrepreneurs

On the following pages, you will meet a group of young men and women—social entrepreneurs—who have fused passion and commitment in support of causes greater than themselves. In doing so, they set in motion a benevolent cycle of recognition, feedback, reinforcement, skill-building and quantifiable success that helped transform not only their lives but also the lives of others.

Chapter

2

Joshua's Closet

"I refused to become another statistic. These girls weren't statistics. They just needed a hand."

—Keiana

It was Christmas Eve when Keiana and her mother, Wanda, arrived home from a routine doctor's appointment. Her father, Antonio, busy with holiday preparations, looked up, a welcoming smile on his face. Keiana flew right past him, tears spilling across her lovely features. A moment later, the door to her room slammed shut with a terrible finality.

"Pregnant," says Antonio, recalling that life-changing moment. "Probably wooed by a young man who got into her ear a little bit."

Keiana was 14 years old at the time, a sheltered child in a religious family, an exuberant, ambitious 9th grader. A cheerleader at Atlanta's The New Schools at Carver, an honor student, a kid, recalls Principal Dr. Darian Jones, "already looking ahead to college." She was naïve beyond her years and, like so many teens, blind to the risks swirling around her.

Despite the warnings and counseling and best efforts, the epidemic of childhood pregnancies is taking a terrible toll. Today, 16 percent of African-American teens become pregnant before their 20th birthday.

Keiana's well-ordered world wobbled dangerously. Antonio was devastated, confusing a daughter's grief over hurting her parents with his own anger and frustration. "We'd been very, very close all our lives," he says. "I thought she'd confide in me. I'd always been there for her." A lament familiar to every parent who discovers there are aspects of their children's lives and behavior forever closed to them.

Perhaps it was the first stirrings of life burgeoning within her or her religious faith and family values, but a spark was kindled. Keiana decided against an abortion. It smoldered for three months—a time of tears, recrimination, introspection and finally, acceptance—and then flickered to life. Keiana, Antonio and Wanda had struggled to keep the pregnancy secret and fooled no one. At the Love Fellowship Christian Church, Pastor Darryl Thomas and his close-knit congregation "sensed something was wrong," Antonio recalls, "but didn't know what." "Acceptance," he says, "opened the floodgates. We were released and began to move forward."

Keiana stayed in school. No easy thing when 49 percent of all teenage mothers drop out. She endured the whispers, giggles and cutting jokes. She sensed the unspoken judgment "of another promising kid likely to come to nothing" in the eyes of some of her teachers. "I refused to become another statistic," she recalls. And for the first time, she noticed the other pregnant girls and teenaged mothers in the shadows of the bustling magnet school, and she felt the shock of recognition. Children themselves, they were outcasts. Some had been abandoned by their families. Others were already slipping into the cycle of dependency that had trapped their mothers and grandmothers before them. The fathers were of little help or were nowhere to be found.

Keiana gave birth to Joshua on August 13, 2008, the first day of her sophomore year, missing six weeks of school. Returning to class, the solid A and B student was shocked to receive her first C grade. A once-untroubled adolescence was being torn apart by fear, uncertainty and crushing responsibility. She wasn't just isolated, she felt invisible like those other pregnant girls she'd seen at The New Schools at Carver. "I'd been a cheerleader," she recalls. "I couldn't cheer anymore. My friends stopped talking to me. I was all by myself, lonely and depressed."

What spark inspired Keiana to turn her life around? Who can really say why some adolescents, finding themselves at the brink of despair and destruction, rally and transform themselves? Why others plunge—despite our best efforts—into the abyss? Or why one generation is deemed the greatest, while another is decried as self-absorbed? Keiana had Joshua, a healthy, bouncing boy. She was young, otherwise unscarred by life. Her faith was strong. Her parents rallied from their own disappointment to support her, but there was still a gaping hole in her life. School and parenting, important as they were, could not bridge the gap.

Joshua's closet was filling up with onesies, disposable diapers, toys, powders and shampoos, gifts from her parents and church friends. Simple acts of kindness multiplied, carrying Keiana back to those other teen mothers who had so little support. She saw them much more clearly now: shadows in the school corridors, girls in thin coats huddling with their babies at bus stops in the morning chill, desperate children forced to move from place to place, lacking the barest knowledge of motherhood and seemingly incapable of its responsibilities.

Ultimately, she recognized yet another girl, this one staring back at her in the mirror. "I can't say I knew or understood every one of them," Keiana recalls, "but I knew what they were going through. We were the same." In that moment, pain transformed into passion and purpose. It was the first stirrings of commitment.

Antonio, who routinely worked two jobs to support his family, was in for yet another surprise. "She came to me one day," he recalls, "and said, 'Dad, can I give away some of the diapers and stuff we've been keeping?' "

"What?"

" 'And some of the clothes I've been getting?' "

He had his doubts, but when Keiana explained what she wanted to do, they faded. "Yeah...Okay...Great...Do it."

" 'Love you Dad!' "

So Keiana started taking out some of the gifts she'd received for Joshua and giving them to the young ladies.

It was a transformative act. Providing help and support to pregnant teens became a driving force in Keiana's life. There would be no standing adrift as the world passed her by. "I wasn't a statistic," she says. "These girls weren't statistics. All they needed was a hand."

Antonio says there was always an ambitious, goal-driven side to his daughter. One day, out of the blue, she'd announced she wanted to become a pediatrician. A banner, The Raven Center for Pediatric Child Care, appeared over her bed (Antonio's doing) to keep her eyes on the prize. When she attended Ralph J. Bunche Middle School, she had hawked candy, raising money for other peoples' causes. All she needed was a cause

Returning to class, the solid A and B student was shocked to receive her first C grade.

of her own.

Joshua's Closet was no closet at all, but a dream coaxed painstakingly to life. GivingPoint helped Keiana create a nonprofit, providing mentoring, support and, ultimately, the recognition adolescents need from the adult world. A registered 501(c)3 nonprofit organization dedicated to parenting teenage mothers, Joshua's Closet sat on a corner in East Point, Georgia. The brick building with double doors and windows smiled expectantly onto the sidewalk. It was on a street so quiet that on Friday nights in autumn you could hear the thump and percussion of the Tri-Cities High School marching band urging their beloved Bulldogs on to victory.

Inside the building, Joshua and Keiana spent many hours rummaging among supplies of diapers, strollers, playpens, bathtubs, powders and lotions, the endless and costly necessities of childbirth. She distributed these at no cost to expectant young mothers, all of them unmarried. More than 150 girls have passed through the welcoming doors in the last few years. What began essentially as a diaper and baby powder giveaway (Keiana and Antonio still go door to door seeking sponsors) expanded into a full-service array of parenting, nutrition, job training, financial literacy and counseling instruction, taught by professionals made available through the local (Fulton County) government. Keiana demands one thing of her girls, the same challenge she had: They must stay in school.

She graduated 7th in her class at the very competitive The New Schools at Carver. It was just the beginning of her journey. Joshua's Closet also became the impetus for her being selected a Gates Millennium Scholar (funded by a grant from the Bill & Melinda Gates Foundation), which meant a full ride to the college of her choice.

At GivingPoint, we realize that selflessness like Keiana's is not an isolated act unique and apart in an uncaring universe. It sets in motion a cycle of commitment and positive reinforcement that leads to transformation. If there is a moral to the story, it's that in high school, as in life, success, even transcendence, is not solely the domain of the athlete, artist, scholar, or social butterfly. It has to do with getting involved. As President Theodore Roosevelt said more than a century ago:

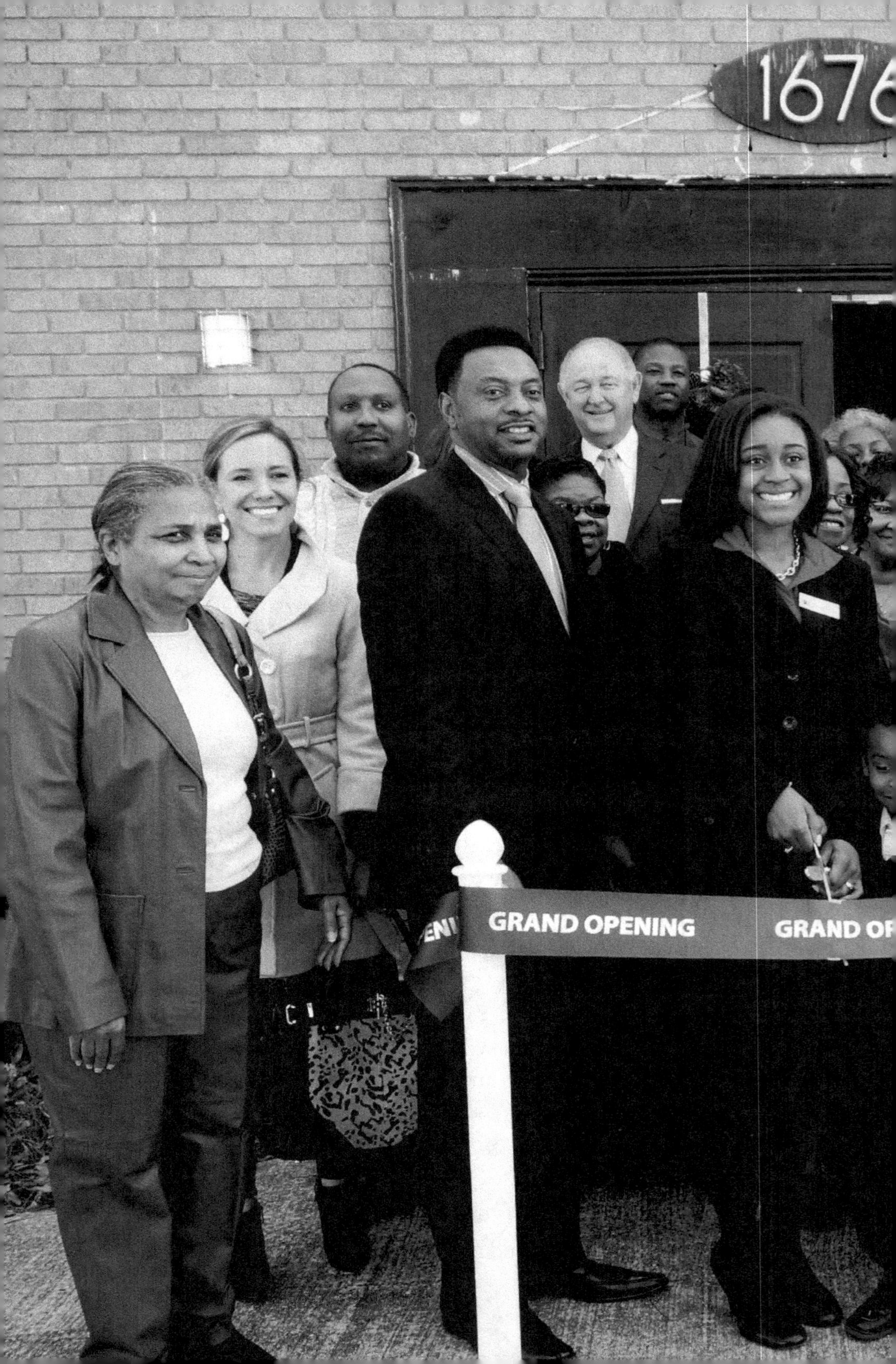
1676
GRAND OPENING
GRAND OP

"...the credit belongs to the man who is actually in the arena...who knows great enthusiasms, the great devotions, who spends himself in a worthy cause..."

Adolescence in urban Atlanta is gritty and unpredictable. In 2013, another The New Schools at Carver student, despondent over an unwanted pregnancy, took her own life. Rumors have it that the girl hanged herself in her closet. Of course, word rippled back to Keiana. "She would have been one of my girls. Maybe I could have..." In the words of Vietnam-era nurse Lola McGourty, who learned painfully, "Sometimes you can't stop the bleeding."

Keiana has now graduated from Atlanta's Spelman College with a degree in economics and is thinking about grad school. She knows she didn't come this far alone. Long before she came to our attention at GivingPoint, The New Schools at Carver Principal Dr. Darian Jones and Dr. Lateshia Woodley, a psychologist who'd been a teen mom herself, served as mentors and role models. They, too, surely had a spark in their lives.

Absent passion for those needy and invisible child-moms and her willingness to commit herself to them, what could have been a tale of missed opportunities and throwaway lives was, instead, a transformation. In a very real way, Keiana experienced not only the birth of her son, but also the rebirth of her soul.

Chapter

3

Give a

Birthday

As a child, Jaya journeyed to India to visit her grandparents. She was the daughter of an engineer and a psychiatrist. A girl who'd never really wanted for anything. Now, she found herself awash in a sea of desperation, her Western clothes a beacon on streets teeming with starving children who looked so much like her. Even at age 8, she had to do something. "My mom would give me money to go buy things," she recalls. "I'd give it away to poor people who'd walk up to me. In India, this is so common."

"Jaya, you can't do this every time," her mom would gently scold. "You can't pay off all of them. There will always be poor people in the streets." Jaya's parents, Sanjay and Sunita, knew this intimately, because they had pulled themselves out of poverty, working their way through school to give Jaya and her brother, Anshul, a better life. Sanjay spent years clerking in a convenience store, not the best training for an electrical engineer. Sunita barely survived a toxic cloud of chemicals that killed more than 10,000 people in Bhopal, India, the world's worst industrial disaster. Her family lost everything.

"Education is the key to success." Jaya constantly heard this refrain from her parents, uncles and aunts. A dutiful daughter, she studied hard, did well, but there was something about those desperate children with their outstretched hands. A spark had somehow leaped from the bitter ashes of their lives onto her soul. "I can't bear other people suffering," she says. "I don't know why I'm this way, but I know I'll always be."

By the time she reached her senior year at Milton High School, Jaya was an academic star dreaming of Ivy League schools and a career in finance and technology. A member of the National Honor Society and Future Business Leaders of America, she moved easily among all the tribal cliques and clans that flourish in high school. Jaya was the go-to girl when anyone had a question about dreaded college essays or convoluted applications. So much so, that one week she was bombarded with 50 texts from students seeking her advice. "I don't get mad," she says. "I probably

She's especially drawn to needy children whose hopes and dreams should be as vibrant as her own.

have the answer, and I'm easier to figure out than a college website."

Ironically, at Alpharetta Elementary, Jaya spent years as the only student of Indian descent. (A teacher once confiscated the nan bread her mom packed for lunch deeming it nutritionally inappropriate.) Today, she encounters another irony. Her friends from Johns Creek, a big south Asian enclave, are uncomfortable with the fact she has so many Caucasian friends.

"How do you fit in so easily?" they ask. "How are you so involved in that culture?"

"They're just like us," Jaya shrugs. "They're people."

Jaya cares about people, particularly those less privileged. She's especially drawn to needy children whose hopes and dreams should be as vibrant as her own. She spent years volunteering, doing the usual round of cleanups and make-work projects that all students suffer through. "I went to all the little places," she says, "but there was something missing. I never got any human interaction."

One day at the North Fulton Community Charities Center, everything changed. "When I arrived, there was a huge line around the building," she recalls. "Inside, everyone was sitting, waiting for bread. Just a piece of bread! There were children crying everywhere. 'Only one piece?' a little boy questioned in a really sad voice. That hit me so hard."

The spark she carried ignited the fire of passion and commitment. "I wasn't 18," Jaya says. "I wasn't even 16, but I needed to do things that connected me to real people. Sometimes, it's painful." While volunteering at North Fulton Community Charities, she overheard this scrap of conversation between a little girl and her mother:

Girl: "Mom, I want this tiara thing for my birthday party."

Mom: "We can't. Let's skip the party this year, OK? We can go to the park."

Girl: "Mom, please...."

The scene unfolded again. This time it was between Jaya's mother's secretary and the secretary's young daughter. As Jaya recalls, "Samantha started telling me how her daddy died in a car accident in California, and they had to move to Georgia to live with a family friend. Her mom couldn't afford to do anything for her birthday."

With both mothers' approval, Jaya organized a party at the Wills Park pavilion in Alpharetta. "It was a short, small thing," she remembers. "Eight kids from her school, cake, pizza. But I could see how much fun Samantha had, and her mom was so thankful." Jaya sensed that other children, certainly children who were homeless, were being denied the same simple joy. She decided to try to make a difference in at least some of their lives.

The challenge was leveraging her initial success. "I've got an entrepreneurial personality," Jaya says, "and it struck me, Social Entrepreneurship! I would start a nonprofit that raises money to throw birthday parties for kids in homeless shelters."

Give A Birthday! was born.

To her dismay, Jaya encountered a wall of well-meaning naysayers. "So much criticism," she remembers, "coming from my family, friends, my uncles and aunts, even one of my teachers. They said, 'Birthday parties don't do any good for these children. They need food, shelter and education.'" Her peers, busy with the demands society makes of affluent adolescents, shrugged her off saying, "Oh, such a cute little idea, but why would you spend your time like that?"

"I didn't have any answer at first," Jaya admits. And there were other pressing issues such as how to raise money, attract attention, refine her message, approach the homeless shelters, convince classmates and friends to volunteer, work out schedules and negotiate the myriad legal complexities of setting up a 501(c)3 nonprofit corporation. There were the nut-and-bolt complexities of cakes, balloons, goody bags, transportation and uncooperative weather. As she struggled, a classmate suggested that GivingPoint, a go-to resource for budding social entrepreneurs, could provide the skills and training she'd need to make Give A Birthday! a success.

On the strength of her dedication and power of her idea, Jaya was invited to join the GivingPoint Institute (GPI). GPI constantly tries to identify students who demonstrate a strong commitment to service and civic engagement. It pairs them with high-profile mentors and role models who assist with their community service projects, bringing real-world knowledge, experience, and expertise to bear. Business planning, marketing, public relations, fund-raising, even crisis management are part of the GPI agenda.

Many of Jaya's concerns were addressed at a GPI seminar hosted by Goldman Sachs. "People asked what Give A Birthday! does and I said, 'We go to homeless shelters and do birthday parties for kids.' Now I realize it's so much more than that. The Goldman Sachs presentation taught me to refine the elevator message, or what the idea really represents."

In doing so, Jaya distilled the essence of Give A Birthday! "Sure, these children need food, education and shelter," she says. "But they also need a boost of self-esteem. The focus of Give A Birthday! is the human need to feel valued and special."

After a kickoff party at the Drake House in Roswell, (a shelter for abused women), any doubts vanished. "They wrote thank-you cards and invited us to come back," Jaya says. "All my volunteers were excited. Everybody was crying happy tears." In recent months, Give A Birthday! has hosted five other parties at the Ronald McDonald House Charities, The Garden in Smyrna, and The Drake House. Each of them was a logistical nightmare, but also a rousing success.

To underwrite her work, she's raised thousands of dollars from family, friends, local businesses and other nonprofits, most recently to include a $1,000 *PutYourPassionToAction* Award from GivingPoint. A number of positive stories in the Atlanta Journal Constitution and other area newspapers brought attention and further donations. Ever the entrepreneur, Jaya petitioned the Future Business Leaders of America at Milton High to list Give A Birthday! among its approved charities. (Student donors earn membership points for their gifts.) "It was one of my savvy ideas," she says with a wink. "We got a huge collection of supplies without having to buy them."

Ultimately, even the critics who complained that parties don't do any good for children with such deep-rooted problems have quieted. "This was the part that killed me," Jaya says, "because I'm super into education. Now I try to combine both. Whenever we host a party, we give the person in charge of the shelter a huge bag of books, binders, pencils and whatnot to distribute among the kids when school starts. Everyone is happy with that."

Give A Birthday! is more than a charity for underprivileged kids. It is the spark that not only will ignite a candle on a birthday cake but also will light up a child's heart and make him feel valued and special.

Chapter

4

Ageless

interAction

"These older adults are totally normal people.

My own classmates, these young people, don't believe they are!" —Meagan

In 2005, an exceedingly bright 15-year-old girl named Meagan arrived at Lassiter High School in East Cobb County, Georgia. She'd transferred from a very small private school in Indianapolis where she says she had been a happy, well-adjusted member of the student body. The uprooting was an unintended, but familiar, consequence of her father's career travels, an arc that curved so dramatically that even a decade later, Meagan is still not certain what he does.

"Something with computers?" she shrugs.

At Lassiter, she was the new kid, moving from a school with perhaps 200 students to Lassiter's overwhelming 2,000-plus student body. She was an instant outsider. "Everybody seemed to know one another from preschool," she recalls. "Their parents knew each other. They all went to the same churches."

"It was really hard to figure out where I fit," Meagan continues. "My freshman year, I ate lunch in the library every day." She focused on her studies, joined a book club. As for athletics, she picked the loneliest sport: long-distance running. Years later, her high school years remain mostly a blur. "I was the wallflower," she remembers. "The quiet mouse who did her work."

Something else was at work in her, an unformed but deeply rooted desire to make a difference. This was the spark that would carry Meagan far beyond the outsider's loneliness and the high school stereotypes of mice, wallflowers, jocks, cheerleaders, stoners and nerds. It lay dormant

all the years her father was "the go-to guy everyone calls" when there was a problem. It was in her grandmother who lived on the outskirts of New Delhi. When Meagan traveled to India for a visit, she'd noticed her granny never ignored the homeless and needy souls lining the alleys and roadways. Her grandmother made a point of sharing what little she had.

A drop in the ocean, but it registered with a young girl trying to find herself. Meagan also had a basic understanding of her religion, Jainism, an ancient faith that teaches the sanctity of all living things.

Lassiter High School is a brick and glass structure sitting approximately 35 miles north of The New Schools at Carver, Keiana's alma mater. The school ranks 14th in Georgia and 428th nationally according to *U.S. News & World Report* surveys. Its student body reflects the surrounding environs of an overwhelmingly middle class and a smattering of affluent as well as economically disadvantaged students. Twenty-four percent are minority, and a growing number are from India, China and Korea.

Lassiter fields powerhouse sports teams. Its male and female athletes have captured 28 state championships since 1980, among them lacrosse, swimming, gymnastics and softball. It boasts a bruising football team and a baseball squad that claimed a national championship in 1999.

Anyone who has attended a suburban high school in the last quarter century will recognize the familiar drone of its classrooms echoing along polished halls, the distant, tantalizing smell of steam tables in the cafeteria, the bright posters and attractive landscaping, the halls crowded with chattering seemingly carefree students. Taken together, it's a mirror that reflects what is admirable in American public education—and also what is troubling.

Almost invisible among Lassiter's 2,000 students—particularly its academic and athletic standouts, multitudinous club members, cheerleaders and high-stepping band members—are hundreds and hundreds of unheralded adolescents. Kids working on assignments, trying to puzzle out college, the job market or the best way to ask a classmate on a date. Kids heading to afterschool jobs at Arby's or Chick-fil-A, or cruising aimlessly in 5-year-old Hondas outfitted with high-end sound systems and bleating exhausts. Kids who mostly do their homework, make passing grades and stay out of trouble, who have considerable time on their hands and spend too much of it in their rooms or hanging out at the nearby Merchants Walk multiplex or Town Center mall. Kids who are latchkey kids because their parents work along the I-285 corridor, or further north in Alpharetta, or maybe downtown Atlanta. Kids who, if you drew them out (and hardly anyone ever does), would admit they're uncertain, unfulfilled and ill at ease. Kids in whom the bright spark of passion that should illumine their future path may be sputtering or in danger of going dark. Kids who want and need to be acknowledged, but despite the lip service of politicians and overburdened educators, they fall through the cracks, a phrase that does not capture the pain of an unfulfilled life. Kids like Meagan.

Their busy, busy parents wonder what they are up to and what can be done to get them interested and excited about the world they're soon to be part of. Or in the absolute worst scenarios, they wonder how to keep them from becoming a story we all dread seeing on cable news.

Parents who say, "How did we, who meant so well, go so wrong?"

At Lassiter, Meagan began doing volunteer work, serving as a teacher's assistant at Bells Ferry Elementary School. She experienced an unexpected rush of happiness seeing the kids' unabashed need for human contact, their smiley faces and outsized excitement. It was far more satisfying than chasing an elusive 4.0 GPA and, as it turned out, more predictive of what would become Meagan's passion.

The spark blossomed into a flame a few years later at Georgia State University (GSU) in downtown Atlanta. GSU is a school where faculty members often have real-world jobs and hands-on expertise they're eager to share. No ivory tower, GSU has a reputation for doing, not pondering. As a freshman, she found herself at a volunteer fair in which nonprofit organizations showed up to recruit students. Meagan, who grew up in a suburb where bad things rarely happened and certainly were not spoken of, volunteered to work in a hospice. The long days spent in hospice would change her life and the lives of others—young and old—she would encounter.

"At first, it was purely companionship," she says. "I'd sit with an older adult to provide friendship. It's important because a lot of the time, dying people lose their friendship circles and become isolated. Some days, I was there to give another caregiver respite or to make a run to the grocery store."

Just like the way our eyes adjust to things in a dark room, Meagan began to see things she'd missed. "There's a calmness that people acquire over a lifetime," she recalls. "When you get to your 70s, 80s, and 90s, you have so much insight. There's no need to impress anybody. You are who you are, and you have all these years of life experience.

"After a while, I started talking about my life and what I was going through. I'd never looked at myself through the lens of an 87- or 91-year-old, but when you see death approaching, you understand life is not permanent, it's a feeble, fickle thing. So you appreciate it that much more. These conversations really changed me," she says.

"Margaret" was Meagan's second hospice patient. In her 80s, with an outsized personality, Margaret had been diagnosed with lung cancer, but she continued chain-smoking. "Honey, my old doctor told me cigarettes would help me with anything," she would say. "No one is going to tell me different!"

Illness cracked that feisty independence. Margaret was forced to move into an assisted-living facility, an efficiency apartment with a small kitchen she tried to make her own. Though widowed for years, she had hung a photograph of her husband, dashing in his WWII uniform, outside her bedroom. "Margaret was faithful until the day she died," Meagan remembers. "So much love really moved me. She was in love with him and her family."

As is often the case, Margaret's family was a family in name only. Her only daughter traveled around the country a lot. She wasn't close to her grandchildren. Meagan remembers Margaret saying, "I wish I'd done more. But I know they're busy, and it's so hard to make time."

The truths Margaret couldn't put into words were not lost on Meagan. "Our families are disintegrating in front of our eyes and with them our history, traditions and values," she says. "What has replaced them? DVD discs on dusty machines that are never played?"

For months, Meagan visited Margaret every Saturday morning and didn't leave until late in the afternoon. Margaret would dress up for these meetings, dabbing on makeup, doing her thinning hair, applying a touch of her favorite perfume. "She always wanted to look good," Meagan recalls. "At the end, it became more difficult."

Meagan spent hours fluffing pillows for the emaciated woman, helping her put on layers of clothes when the chill was in her bones, wincing at her gasps. Most importantly, she listened to the old woman's stories. Margaret had lived through the Great Depression, World War II, the Civil Rights Era, drawing truth and knowledge well beyond her years.

Those long afternoons, Meagan left the apartment neither bummed nor depressed, but feeling awesome. "Visiting Margaret gave me this indescribable feeling of accomplishment, I can't compare it with anything," she says. Years later, the woman remains the most memorable person Meagan has ever known. Certainly the most vital and "so confident in her abilities, thoughts and opinions."

Meagan's transformation was complete when it struck her how close this amazing person had come to dying alone and abandoned. She chose gerontology as her major and discovered there were millions of other

Margarets out there warehoused in nursing homes and assisted-living facilities, many in terrible straits. As the baby boomer generation ages, there will be millions more, even as an epidemic of Alzheimer's disease spreads across the globe.

She discovered that it barely mattered if the aging lived in gilded suites with every amenity or in rundown, barebones facilities. If they felt lonely and ignored, it wasn't comfort they craved, it was human interaction. Needing little, they had so much to give in return.

She had to share what she'd learned. Though idealistic and spiritual, possessed of a big heart, scant money and a crushing workload, what could she do? "My struggle was to convince a 17-year-old would-be volunteer that hanging out with an 87-year-old is cool," she remembers. "How do I find the means to turn that passion on?"

By her junior year, passion defined Meagan. She'd visited many other assisted-living communities, ever more convinced something was very wrong. "When I'm 87, I don't want to be playing Bingo or singing "Rock-a-Bye Baby." It's infantile. Too many of these activities are demeaning. They lacked human connection. Worse, these older adults are totally normal people, and these young people, my classmates, wouldn't believe they were," Meagan says.

"There was this disconnect," she continues. "How could I get people talking to one another? There's this huge wealth of knowledge and understanding out there and no way to communicate it to young people." Meagan started an Adopt-a-Grandparent program (today, a funded and chartered campus organization) as a platform for college students to build one-to-one friendships with aging adults.

She graduated from Georgia State, still unsatisfied that she was getting the message out. She even planned to take a year off "to party and be a 22-year-old kid," but she couldn't do it. She realized that passion alone is not enough to transform lives. She had no idea how a nonprofit worked. She needed mentoring, networking, and, certainly, resources. With GivingPoint's support and guidance, Meagan created a nonprofit. She called it Ageless interAction. It took many months for her 501(c)3 nonprofit application to be approved. Grants and student volunteers trickled in, but Meagan's social passion and commitment has only grown stronger. Her dream is to build a national organization with Adopt-a-Grandparent-type programs at different universities, independent but able to tap into the mother ship in Atlanta for resources and guidance.

Meagan has traveled a long way from the isolated high school student she once was. "I've got lots of friends my age" she says. "I never thought I'd enjoy sitting around with older adults, but I do. I know other young people who feel the same way. It's not going to change. Aging is one thing we all have in common, and it is a good thing."

Bridging the generation gap, Meagan has learned that in giving to others, one receives far more in return.

Chapter

5

Simple Math

Today

"I've always had this thing in me. I want to solve problems. If something's out there and it's bothering a lot of people, I'll always dive in and see what I can do to help." – **Uwezo**

As a child, Uwezo was forced to confront a painful truth. The father he loved and admired, whose name he carried, was a restless man with big dreams and great frustrations but was rarely there for him. It's a familiar story, but no less traumatic. Uwezo was also blessed. He had a loving mother who guided him through what might have been a turbulent adolescence, a close-knit, extended family whose values (self-respect, hard work, determination, giving back to one's community) would shape him, and a younger brother, Askari, who relied on him.

Like a character in one of the Swahili folk tales his grandmother shared with him, Uwezo discovered a hidden treasure. Mathematics, the abstract science of numbers, quantity and space that frustrates so many students, was as clear to him as water drawn from a mountain spring. He discovered this gift journeying from the DeKalb County School District to the Atlanta Public Schools (APS), as Cindy Smith, his fiercely protective mother, negotiated the treacherous shoals of inner-city education to find the best schools, the best teachers, the best programs for her two sons.

"I was in the third or fourth grade at Oakcliff Elementary School," Uwezo remembers. "We'd play this game called 24. To win, you had to arrive at 24 using the four numbers on your card. You could add, subtract, multiply or divide, using each number only once. I was able to grasp the concept quickly. It was Pow! Pow! Pow! racing my friends to see who was better. I'd show everybody how I got to 24 and grab the next card."

The winning numbers kept coming, a spark that Uwezo would nurture over the next decade. "It got to a point where I wasn't just recognizing cards," he recalls. "I was able to manipulate and move numbers around exactly how I wanted to." Addition and subtraction expanded into decimals, fractions, algebra, geometry, trigonometry, calculus. "I'd found my niche," he says. "I began to see math as my friend. It was something I was good at that had always been inside me."

In every tale of discovered treasure, unexpected things unfold – opportunities, challenges, setbacks and pitfalls. "Other students began to look up to me," he says grinning. "I guess I craved attention. I was a kid!" Moving from Oakcliff Elementary in DeKalb County to Sammye E. Coan Middle School in Atlanta, Uwezo noticed something else, something that, at first, was satisfying and then troubling. "I was picking up on math way faster than my classmates," he says. "Then I realized we were going over adding and subtracting and sometimes multiplication in the 8th grade. This was stuff that should have been covered in 3rd grade."

At the time, the APS system was being rocked by a massive cheating scandal perpetrated not by students, but by teachers, principals, and administrators at the highest levels. More than 175 Atlanta teachers and principals were discovered altering or otherwise enhancing students' standardized test scores, a criminal violation. Most went on to accept a plea bargain arrangement to avoid jail, but 11 educators were tried and convicted on racketeering and conspiracy charges. Despite their cries of outrage (they claimed they were pressured to meet unrealistic academic standards), the real victims were the students. "Nobody had taken the time to see these kids got the math instruction they needed to be successful," Uwezo says. "Instead, they just kept pushing them through and pushing them through."

At Maynard H. Jackson High School, Uwezo decided he would take the time, a challenge that would not prove easy. "Is there anything I can do?" he asked himself. "Is this bigger than me? Will they have to process a whole new round of teachers?" He found the answers he needed embedded in his own life experiences and the spark he'd nurtured. "My dad taught me that each of us has a connection," he recalls. "If the person next to me needs something, I should help them so they can help me with something else. My mom is about helping everybody. My connection was math."

In the 9th grade, he created Simple Math Today, a tutoring program that allowed him to reach out to other, less-gifted students and help them master basic mathematics. "For a while, I was out there by myself," he says. "Then I realized I could recruit high schoolers to come in and tutor middle schoolers." His approach was as logic-driven as a geometry proof. High school students need community service hours; tutoring satisfies community service. Therefore, "Come with me and you get community service hours." A corollary elevated Uwezo's social entrepreneurism to a higher plane, converting a smoldering spark into a flame that radiated heat (passion) and light (insight). "Suddenly, I could see my connection to math was bigger than just figuring out my place in the world," he recalls. "It wasn't, 'Where do I fit?' but rather, 'How can I share and tutor and teach others?'"

His first stop was Coan Middle School. There, the math coordinator introduced Uwezo to Deshaun, an 8th grader who was struggling, scoring years behind his grade level in math. Deshaun wasn't merely messing up his computations, Uwezo realized, "he didn't even know what procedures to use to work a problem, whether to multiply, divide or subtract." He began working with Deshaun twice a week for three months. "After a while, he started getting the material. I could see he was really enjoying himself!"

Deshaun put his new math skills on display, earning a 90% on a class test, compared with his usual 50% or 60%. Uwezo says, "This was his moment!" Unfortunately, in the real world unexpected things can happen. "His teacher saw such a huge jump," Uwezo says, "and the correlation was that he cheated." A repeat performance and a wake-up call between

"I'd been asking myself, 'Can this be better? Can I extend it to more people? Can I broaden my own horizons?'"

the disbelieving teacher and Uwezo set things straight. "Deshaun showed up with this big smile on his face," Uwezo says. As for the tutor, it was a watershed moment. "A lot of times I work with a student and then have to move on to the next. I don't get to see any results. With Deshaun, I could see my work was an investment that paid off," he says.

Around this time, GivingPoint's Director of Community Outreach was introduced to this smiling, personable young man juggling high school and college math courses, tutoring his peers, heading the Engineering Club, tracking other students' community service hours, printing recruiting fliers, running around arranging transportation for his tutors, all the while trying for a semblance of normal high school life.

Simple Math Today provided entry into GivingPoint. Under the platform, Uwezo's vision expanded exponentially. "At first, tutoring was just something I did," he says. "I'd been asking myself, 'Can this be better? Can I extend it to more people? Can I broaden my own horizons?'" Eventually he applied and was accepted into the GivingPoint Institute (GPI), which provided the missing tools to pursue his goals. "I learned about networking and how the business world works," Uwezo says. He also discovered what he jokingly calls, "speaker lingo," which allowed him to "get in front of a school board and talk to them reasonably about implementing my tutoring program within school hours," he says.

There were GPI field trips and a memorable seminar at the Coca-Cola Company headquarters on target marketing, practical advice on fund-raising and scaling-up his nonprofit's reach via a website and social media. "GivingPoint showed me more efficient ways to get things done," he says. "I wasn't thinking about building a site so people could visit Simple Math Today and practice on worksheets without me actually being there. It was just come here, go there, do that – elementary thinking. I discovered building an interface could be a game changer." Other savvy and selfless young social entrepreneurs – his GivingPoint peers – provided examples and inspiration, crucial to his overall development. He did the same for them.

Adolescent life is rarely a fairy tale. Carrying a full high school academic load, taking advanced math courses at Atlanta Metropolitan State College, growing his tutoring program, working on arcane applications to MIT and other elite schools, Uwezo continued his string of A's in advanced math courses until the spring of 2015.

"I got a D in calculus," he says glumly.

He knew he was struggling. Professors were much more demanding than high school instructors. Uwezo was exhausted and overworked. This was college-level calculus, the bane of generations of pre-med and engineering students. "So I had to buckle down," he says. Perhaps he recalled his grandmother telling him that his name, Uwezo, in Swahili signifies a "desire to accomplish something outstanding and very worthwhile for humanity early in life." Now a Georgia Tech student, his dream is to become an engineer and work for Elon Musk at Tesla Motors. His passion is to prevent climate change from becoming a catastrophic event.

In any event, he hit the books harder. "I took the calculus class over," Uwezo says. "I flipped it and got my A."

For Uwezo, in the calculus of life, he's aiming for an even higher grade.

Chapter

6

Pair2Share

"What if I start an where anyone can give them to people dance shoes?"

organization
donate shoes and
who can't afford

– Juliana

The spark struck Juliana like the flash of Dorothy's ruby slippers in *The Wizard of Oz.* Juliana's family was moving from Alpharetta, Georgia, to Sandy Springs, a closer-in suburb of Atlanta, and she was forced to clean out her overstuffed closet. No easy thing for a 16-year-old with an expansive sense of style and flair. Dance shoes crowded the topmost shelf, a testimony to an enduring passion: the tap shoes she wore when she was 5 years old, ballet slippers, jazz shoes, every kind and color and style. Each pair was embedded with a bright memory, a triumph, a passing setback, a movement mastered, a challenge met.

None of the shoes fit her, and most pairs were in near-new condition. As a young dancer, Juliana would outgrow a pair in six weeks. They'd been a costly expenditure. What to do with them?

"I started brainstorming," she recalls. That's when it struck her, "What if I collect all these shoes from all these dancers who've been accumulating them for many years and give them to people who can't afford dance shoes?"

She recruited her best friends and fellow dancers Meriah and Mekayla, and together they nurtured the spark that would grow and ultimately set the trio apart from thousands of other overworked, ultra competitive and self-involved high schoolers.

Over time, it would transform their priorities, change how they perceived the world around them and how others perceived them. Like dance, it began with small steps and unexpected rewards. A favorite dance teacher shared his struggles growing up gay in a rural Southern town and how his overarching passion for dance transcended every obstacle life threw at him. He now devotes his life to sharing that passion with others, lessons not lost on the girls. "He really wants us to be prepared, not only in the dance world but also in life," says Juliana.

They met young dancers from far less privileged backgrounds who

Juliana   **Mekayla**   **Meriah**

shared the same love of dance, and the three friends decided to do what they could to help others. They called their idea Pair2Share.

"I knew I could get about 50 pairs just from my friends," Juliana says. "We visualized an organization where anyone could donate shoes, and then we would give them to people who couldn't afford dance shoes."

And so they did. Three suburban high school girls from a generation often labeled as being too self-involved to care about anything beyond the frivolous, embarked on a mission to collect and distribute gently used dance shoes to those in need. Pair2Share, like the rabbit hole in *Alice in Wonderland*, opened a new world for the budding social entrepreneurs.

It was a world of puzzling challenges. Dance shoes had to be solicited, collected, sorted, sized, cleaned and inventoried. A distribution system had to be set up, a website launched and development of an outreach program to fund costs, all of which quickly exceeded a typical teenager's regular allowance.

It was a world of rewards beyond anything the trio imagined. There was the connectedness of spiritual, human, artistic, and philanthropy that they forged while striving for a goal that was service-oriented rather than personal; the happiness they felt sharing their passion with others who were less fortunate but equally passionate; the satisfaction as the idea quickly resonated far beyond their schools, dance studios, friends, and social media circles; the feedback they generated when GivingPoint's adult mentors appeared and networks suddenly opened to them; the life lessons they learned and the practical ones like how to start, promote and operate an enterprise (e.g., budget, fundraise, account, inventory, etc.) be it a nonprofit or a future foray in the arena of personal life and career. And finally, the most eloquent of gifts was the kindness and compassion that blossomed in their hearts.

The first year, the girls collected more than 200 pairs of dance shoes and distributed dozens of shoes to peers who had the passion for dance but not the resources. At one point, the Atlanta Ballet (the Atlanta Ballet!) sent them a note requesting ballet slippers. What began as a love for the physical challenges and rewards of dance—one of the most powerful forms of human expression—became a means of transcendence for Juliana, Meriah and Mekayla.

Passion is at the heart of their story. It flows through all of the individuals in this book. Passion, in its purest form, is defined as "a strong feeling of enthusiasm or excitement for something or about doing something." Passion differentiates Juliana, Meriah and Mekayla from many of their peers—many good, well-meaning kids who are drifting through these critical formative years and others who are already slipping onto a darker path.

You can hear passion in their voices—and these are girls with homework and teachers and responsibilities, taking tough courses with all the other pressures in the relentlessly changing and demanding world they inhabit—when they describe, though words cannot really capture, the joy they've discovered and want to share.

"Dance is different every time I get out there," says Meriah who, like Juliana and Mekayla has been a member of the competitive Vibe Performance Company. "During my first years, I was definitely going through the motions, telling myself, 'My foot goes here, my arm goes there.' I wasn't seriously trying to develop my skill or delve into what dance really is," she says.

"Then one day, it hit me. When I'm dancing, I don't have to be anywhere but in the moment. I don't have to think what I'm doing in school or tonight or anytime. It's all about the moment and the specific movement. It's liberating and, after a while, I realized it's applicable to everything in life," she says. For a generation with never-ending demands on its time, how rare and energizing it is to be in the moment.

When Mekayla was a senior at Alpharetta High School, she had just moved with her family to the metropolitan area. She had to adjust to the fact that she no longer had grandparents, uncles, aunts and cousins living across the street. Footnotes, her dance company, became a kind of extended family, a connection based on a shared interest. "I loved my teachers and all my dance friends," she says. "My younger sister was in it, too. So for me and our mom, dance was a major part of our lives."

Mekayla says dancing can "express all the feelings and emotions" adolescents struggle to capture in words: joy, loneliness, loss, anger, exultation, confusion, the uncertainty of living a world that can be cruel, arbitrary and unforgiving. "I've seen people dance after a bad day at school," says Juliana, who, with Meriah and Mekayla, is now attendng the University of Georgia. "They'll do a certain dance and they'll break down in tears because they've connected to their bad day through dance and are dealing with it. Dance reveals how all our emotions connect."

Like a ballet dancer performing a grand jeté, Pair2Share soared beyond the personal to the universal. Three teens were moved to share their blessings with others less fortunate. They did this with grace, hard work and unstated urgency, because among any generation of adolescents, dark and corrosive energies are always at work. "There are people at my school who are not passionate about anything," Meriah admits. "They have nothing to look forward to. Many get into bad things like smoking and drinking and partying all the time because, having lacked passion for so long, they're reaching the point of not knowing what to do with themselves beyond outlaw activities."

As word of their commitment spread, friends and peers began to perceive selflessness as cool. "They completely understood our passion and have been really supportive," Juliana adds. "They are always asking about Pair2Share and offering ways to help us through their contacts in and outside the dance world."

Pair2Share also has its share of froth and humor. The girls' well-intentioned attempt to supply shoes to Moving in the Spirit, a downtown Atlanta youth development program, fizzled when they realized Spirit's contemporary dancers worked barefoot. But their effort did not go unappreciated. Dana Lupton, the company's artistic director, was so impressed that she put the trio in touch with GivingPoint, which ultimately led to an invitation to join the GivingPoint Institute. They were welcomed with mentoring, technological expertise to spread their story exponentially, financing and, most importantly, the human support and encouragement without which nothing can flourish.

Giving away shoes, these three young women stepped into even bigger ones. And they fit quite well.

Chapter

7

Game Givers

Max seems an unlikely superhero. A self-described "nerd," he's tall, gangly, with a mind so energetic his thoughts often outrace his spoken words.

But if we define "hero" as someone who selflessly undertakes a great challenge, Max is as much a hero as the young, idealistic knights whose quests, retold in the Arthurian legends, have fired the passions of millions of young people.

As it turns out, in his spare time, 16-year-old Max does rescue kidnapped princesses, dispatch dragons, break evil spells and restore kingdoms. Videogames fuel Max's soaring imagination and it's no coincidence that his real world exploits—creating Game Givers, a nonprofit that donates games to children's hospitals—parallel classic games like The Legend of Zelda and Super Mario Brothers that involve rescuing those in dire peril.

Max's tale begins not at King Arthur's Round Table or a gaming console, but a hospital ward in Atlanta where his beloved "Nana" was slowly dying of ovarian cancer. "My grandmother and I were really close," Max recalls. "We'd often talk about her treatment and how difficult it was. And she told me she couldn't believe kids my age and younger were going through similar ordeals." Nana's lime green Gameboy helped her during the long hours of chemotherapy. Max soon realized that playing Tetris was more than a game; it was a way to escape her grim reality.

Haunted by a vision of "kids being woken up at three in the morning for treatment, with nothing to take their minds off it," Max decided he would try to help them. "I was lucky enough not to be in their situation, but

"Children's hospitals are busy saving lives," "They don't have the money or resources for distractions like videogame libraries."

I believed I could make a difference in their lives."

The founders of GivingPoint believe there is an innate desire in all of us to do good, to connect with other human beings, and help the less fortunate. Fulfilling this need is absolutely essential to human happiness and well-being. (Max remembers the intense surge of joy he felt during "cancer walks" with his mom...and when he'd helped raise money to buy school uniforms for African children.) However, all too often, selflessness becomes distorted by the demands, pressures and mixed signals of the "real world" as we rush from childhood into adolescence and beyond. Childlike innocence becomes a liability, not a strength.

"Max has always fought for the underdog," says his mother, Ali. "When he was two, he became best friends with someone with diabetes. From that day, if his friend couldn't go trick or treating, or couldn't eat candy or dessert, Max wouldn't have dessert."

The teenaged Max decided he'd share what gave him the most joy: he'd work with the hospitals to put videogames, particularly his favorites from the '80s and '90s, in the hands of thousands of seriously ill children. According to the National Cancer Institute, nearly 16,000 children were diagnosed with cancer in 2014. Tens of thousands more are hospitalized with heart, cerebrovascular and other long term illnesses. "Children's hospitals are busy saving lives," Max says. "They don't have the money or resources for distractions like videogame libraries."

Neither did he. "I can't pay 60 bucks for a game!" he says. In all quests—from Lord of the Rings to Super Mario Brothers—the traveler somehow discovers the skills or guidance he needs to reach a seemingly insurmountable goal. It wasn't Gandalf or Aragorn who appeared at the leafy Galloway School in suburban Atlanta, where Max is a junior, but a representative of GivingPoint who'd heard from Felicia McCrary, the school's director of student life, about one young man's extraordinary penchant for community service.

That critical encounter provided the inspiration and ultimately, the resources that transformed Game Givers from just another clever idea to a passionate vision and finally, reality. Max's nonprofit has raised nearly

$57,000; money used to purchase and distribute more than one thousand video games to children's hospitals and Ronald McDonald Houses throughout Georgia. He's now expanding Game Givers' reach into New England. It all began when he was invited to become part of the elite GivingPoint Institute (GPI), which identifies high school students who demonstrate a strong commitment to service and civic engagement—"social entrepreneurs"—and pairs them with mentors and role models who provide the real world experience and expertise that assures their community service projects can succeed.

"The fact that I could learn finance from a Goldman Sachs person and how to run an organization from the CEO of a big corporation was incredible," Max says. "I learned every single step of the way. By the end of the program, I had so many tools in my tool belt that I could use to my advantage and continue on and on with my charity."

In every quest, there are looming hurdles and obstacles to overcome. Like any noble knight, Max competes in tournaments; these at a local Italian restaurant where he raises the money to purchase the games he donates to Children's Healthcare of Atlanta, Grady Burn Center, the Shepherd Center, Children's Hospital of Georgia (Augusta) and most recently, Boston Children's Hospital. "We charge ten dollars to play video games for a good cause," he says. "If forty or fifty kids show up, that's 500 dollars!" When someone donated a box of retro video games, he was quick to seize the opportunity: "I set up the games at one of our tournaments so parents could come in and pay to play the games they grew up with." He also collects old games "gathering dust on people's shelves" and donates them to hospitals who repurpose them. He's begun to network with the gaming community, including some of the biggest indie developers, some of whom are willing to commit money and resources to such a worthy cause.

As every gamer knows, there is always another level of the game. Max's quest has led him to what may become his life's path. Recently, he attended a three-week social entrepreneurship program at Stanford University. "I was already interested, but I fell in love with social entrepreneurship," he says, his words racing to keep up with his excitement. "I'm doing what

I'm doing with the charity, but I also want to create a business, make it successful and keep it socially responsible. GivingPoint teaches that if you have a passion, go for it regardless of your age. In fact, use your age to your advantage."

Super Max has done exactly that—to everyone's advantage.

Part

III

The

Parents

"There's no single effort more radical in its potential for saving the world than transforming the way we raise our children." – **Marianne Williamson**

P arents bear a staggering responsibility. We must raise the generation that will one day inherit the world. Inculcate life skills, engender values and virtues, nurture self-esteem, guide our offspring past temptations and pitfalls, all the while pursuing careers, assembling households, setting aside our own dreams to build that elusive but vital construct, the family.

We attempt these arduous tasks in a world dramatically different from the era in which we came of age, exponentially different from the world of our parents. Grandmother, long the font of childrearing wisdom and hands-on experience, no longer lives across the street. For many of us, our notions of parenting derive from gauzy or painful memories, whoever replaced Dr. Spock as the current parenting guru, PBS or the Cartoon Network. If we are brutally honest, our parenting ends up being whatever we did to get past yesterday.

Our task is made more difficult because of ongoing shifts in society. According to American Psychological Association figures, between 40-50 percent of U.S. marriages will end in divorce. The numbers are worse when we marry a second time. Many parents don't marry at all. Three-quarters of all women without college degrees now give birth out of wedlock and suffer all the individual and societal costs. GivingPoint's Keiana, pregnant at 14, whom you know from Chapter 2, went on to finish college and to accomplish great things. She's the exception, not the rule.

We mean well. We want the best for our children. We sacrifice for them. But too often, we neglect to teach them the value of sacrificing for others. And so, they miss the joy and fulfillment, the reward of being a part of something bigger than themselves. And they may spend much of their lives searching for it.

On the following pages are four parents: Vince Coppola, Cindy Smith and her fiance, Louis McNeil and Cindy Abel. They share some of the challenges, sacrifices, insights and joys they encountered on the long road to parenthood. These are personal stories, but you'll find them familiar, if not universal. As you read, ponder the deeper question: In a world rocked by exponential change, when the family as we've understood it for millennia is either evolving or disintegrating, what can we do to supplement and support our parents and children? This is the challenge GivingPoint was created to help address.

Chapter

8

Selflessness

"I tried to shield my son from the pain and inequities of life. We escaped neither." —Vince Coppola

V ince Coppola divorced when his son, Thomas, was 2 years old. Pressured by the issues that undermine so many new marriages—finances, unrealistic expectations, career setbacks—Thomas's mom simply scooped their little boy up and moved back to Virginia. Of course, it was more complicated and messy than that. Every broken marriage has its particular set of dysfunctions and disappointments.

Those months without his son forced Vince to reexamine his priorities. "I swore when he returned, I'd be the best father," he recalls. "In fact, I was a much better father than I'd been a husband."

In the years that followed, father and son spent endless time together. On weekends, Vince never hired a babysitter, never went on a date, never remarried. He read to Thomas, watched a thousand cartoons and movies, hunted down the coolest Transformers the moment they hit the toy stores, shared stories of his childhood and his parents who'd passed away before Thomas was 5 years old.

Around the house, Vince never allowed Thomas to lift a finger. Never questioned whether his own childhood experiences translated in the new and vastly different world Thomas inhabited. He never gave his son permission to attempt anything beyond what was easy and enjoyable. What kid wouldn't want that?

No one teaches us how to parent. Vince's hands-off parenting (Thomas' mom was even more indulgent) seemed to work. Thomas earned good grades, never was a discipline problem. If he spent too much time alone playing video games in his room, what boy didn't? Time passed. Feeling a tingle of uncertainty about what he calls his son's "lackadaisical" disinterest in sports and social activities, Vince enrolled Thomas in a parochial school "to instill religious values, make some new friends, get some structure."

For high school, Vince switched course and enrolled Thomas in a well-regarded private school where the focus was more on individual initiative and personal responsibility. Thomas did well academically, but he wasn't much of a joiner. He didn't participate in Paideia's extensive environmental stewardship, volunteerism or civic involvement programs. "He hasn't found his passion," Vince assured himself. In fact, Vince didn't discover journalism, which he pursued as a means of helping others, until he was nearly 30 years old. "Everyone is different. Boys mature more slowly than girls. He'll find it in college." Looking back, Vince saw he'd been making excuses for his son.

When it came time for college, Thomas was not enthusiastic. "I told him over and over that college would provide him with opportunities to travel, see things, and meet great new people," Vince recalls. "I picked the schools, walked him through his applications, worked on his essays." He pauses, then adds, "I was proud that I could provide my son with material things I never had. But I just couldn't provide the spark he really needed."

Thomas wanted to stay in Atlanta. Vince chose Hamilton College, a leafy private college in upstate New York that ranked near the top academically. The fact that Thomas had never spent time away from home, that brutal winters left the campus buried in snow, and the remnants of a bully-boy fraternity system were still in place, didn't register. Why would it? Vince was too busy architecting his son's life.

Off Thomas went. Vince scrambled to cover tuition, shipped him packages of his favorite foods, books and treats. From his vantage point in the bleachers, things seemed great. For three years, Thomas made the Dean's List, got elected to the honor court, won a public speaking contest and was seemingly on his way to medical school. On the ground, it was a very different story; one Vince is still piecing together. Thomas was painfully shy, socially inept, popular with his professors, but among his peers, he was a loner.

Six weeks from graduation, Thomas dropped out. He got in his car—a car his dad had picked out and helped pay for—and drove 1,000 miles back home. "Thomas had spent his college years thinking he had to please me," Vince says. "It was the wrong message for a parent to send. Honestly, I hadn't given him the direction and guidance he really needed. Providing a free ride through life is very different from being a positive role model and parenting by example."

Thomas stayed in his room for three weeks, wouldn't say much, refused to see a therapist or a counselor. Vince's fears and concerns shaded into disappointment and anger. They clashed. Thomas moved in with his mom. Father and son didn't speak for five months.

The sixth month, Thomas, trying to find himself, enlisted in an infantry unit headed to Iraq. Vince found himself on a parade ground at Fort Benning watching his only son march off to war. "I suffered through weeks when I was afraid to answer the door, and I jumped every time the phone rang," Vince recalls. "Sure enough, bad things happened—war is what it is—but, thank God, not the worst thing."

Thomas spent weeks in an army hospital in El Paso, Texas, and eventually was honorably discharged from the army. He went back to Hamilton College and graduated with honors. He's home now using his army savings as a deposit on a condo and his educational benefits to hopefully work his way into the job market.

Father and son talk every day. They struggle. They move forward. It's not easy or fast. Nothing unfolds according to any parent's plan. Someone said, "Man decides, God laughs," and there's a lot of truth in that. Our children are separate beings, not extensions of us. That's a good thing. Parenting is not done by dictate, but by example. And the best example is selflessness by caring for others less able to care for themselves.

Asked what he might have done differently, Vince insists, "I couldn't have loved him more." Most parents feel this way. Yet, his own life provides a clue, if not the answer. As a reporter in the 1980s, Vince worked among

young men and women dying of AIDS, one of them the brother for whom Thomas is named. He'd met doctors, nurses and volunteers who never hesitated to step forward to combat that terrible disease. Throughout his career, Vince met selfless, passionate men and women again and again in cancer wards, homeless shelters, research labs and military hospitals. In many ways, they were his teachers.

"I should have engendered in my son the compassion and concern I saw in others," he says, "something best done by consistent example, not preaching, planning or writing checks. Most importantly, I should have given Thomas permission—my blessings and encouragement—to engage the larger world with volunteerism and service. Instead, I tried to shield him from the pain and inequities of life. We escaped neither."

A wise man once said, "Words are cousins to deeds." Parenting in a changing world requires that we be role models—not in name, but in deeds. We who are blessed with children must engender passion, commitment and selflessness. There is no more important or rewarding role. If we do so, our children and their children will transform the world.

What could make a parent prouder?

Chapter

Awareness

"I taught my boys how to do a parent conference in the 4th grade and I haven't done one since. They know what my expectations are. If there's a problem with grades, you meet with the teacher. It's your grade. It's your work."

– Cindy Smith, program director,
United Brothers and Sisters of America

At a time when 'helicopter parents' hover over their child's every step, compelled to assure their offspring's academic social success, popularity, confidence and well-being, Cindy Smith's words seem absolutely heretical. Then you meet her sons, Uwezo and Askari – two of the more poised, popular, likeable, selfless and overachieving high schoolers you'll ever encounter – and you wonder about your own overprotective parenting and what gives Smith the right to have such faith not only in their success but also the success of thousands of other sons and daughters.

You discover United Brothers and Sisters of America (UBSA). It's the Atlanta nonprofit Smith and Louis McNeil founded in 2009 in the belief young people can transform themselves and their communities through awareness, service-learning and volunteerism. Today, UBSA, a GivingPoint affiliate, mentors more than 7,000 Atlanta middle and high

school students in afterschool service-learning programs. In turn, these students have birthed thousands of vibrant community service projects.

Not surprisingly, UBSA's goals precisely align with Smith's notion of parenting. It's more complicated than smothering children in unconditional love, and it requires more than running around telling your child when to get up, when to lie down and when do everything. Successful parenting, in Smith's experience, is openness, honesty, instilled values, consistency, trust, faith, passion, service and, ultimately, engendering a commitment to something greater than oneself.

Educators committed to building community, Smith and her fiancé, UBSA cofounder Louis McNeil, moved to Atlanta from DeKalb County hoping to transform their vision of service-learning into concrete reality. Unfortunately, they discovered few transcendent values in programs being offered in the Atlanta public schools. "Students were inside the schools, doing things like stacking books," Smith remembers. "They weren't doing real community service."

This is the same gap between words and deeds that inspired the founding of GivingPoint: Too many young people bursting with untapped energy and passion forced to engage in dull, repetitive make-work projects simply to fulfill a community service requirement for graduation.

Smith and McNeil's vision is much more expansive. "The community service model is the process of investigating and understanding what's going on in the community versus just showing up for a day of service and forgetting it," she says. "When you're involved with something you care about week after week and working with your peers, it becomes a learning process; something you're never going to forget."

Transformation – what GivingPoint labels "the secret sauce" – occurs as students discover their service has real-world, measurable impact. Smith's elder son, Uwezo, for example, created Simple Math Today, a successful tutoring program that helps struggling students master basic mathematics (see Chapter 5).

As so many successful GivingPoint students have discovered, selflessness is not the same as sacrifice. When you believe you can

Transformation occurs as students discover their service has real-world, measurable impact.

transform the world, you are transformed. "Kids don't know they can make a difference," says Smith. "When they learn about something, commit themselves to it, and see results, it changes them."

Unfortunately, visionary ideas often tend to sink into the morass of bureaucracy. When Smith and McNeil approached the Atlanta Board of Education (recently wracked by a cheating scandal that drew national headlines), the initial response was, "Please don't make the teachers create one more thing!"

Undaunted, they created a turnkey program. "We understood that teachers don't have the time to seek out resources and put together lesson plans on homelessness, recycling, HIV/AIDS or whatever civic topic for an after-school program," Smith says. "We answered all their questions and built everything into a package that was presentable, easy to offer and easy for teachers to facilitate."

Of course, the program wasn't enough. No angel arrived to underwrite the time and effort needed to seed and grow and validate UBSA. So Smith and McNeil made the leap of faith that's often necessary to ensure real success. "We funded it out of our own pocket," she says with a laugh. "For years, we wanted to prove that students would be engaged, parents would be involved and teachers would be excited about doing something like this."

They also wanted to ensure that when it became imperative to fund-raise (very few people can underwrite a nonprofit, however worthy, indefinitely), they would have results that proved the UBSA model viable and impactful. "We didn't want to say, 'We're thinking about this.' Rather, it was, 'This is what we've done. We know it works. You should support this.'"

Enter Askari, Smith's second son, a dynamo pumping out positive energy and good intentions in all directions. Like his brother, Uwezo, Askari is one of the self-selected overachievers chosen to be part of the GivingPoint Institute. GPI identifies students who demonstrate a passion for service and civic engagement and pairs them with high-profile mentors who assist with their community service projects, applying real-world

Cindy Smith

Louis McNeil

knowledge, experience and expertise.

Given the tools, there was little doubt how Askari would apply them. "He saw that UBSA students lacked the resources to grow their projects," Smith remembers, "and he took on the challenge of finding funding for United Brothers and Sisters of America by himself."

Askari handed out fliers on the sidewalk to raise a few bucks, and he hosted a "dine-out" at The Pullman, a local restaurant, hustling and cajoling until 50 people, including two teachers, agreed to show up. One of the diners was then-Mayor of Atlanta, Shirley Franklin, so something was in the air. The mentoring he'd received at GPI began to kick in. "GPI gave me confidence and real-world knowledge," he says. "It gave me a sense of what networking really is, what a project should really be about and how to make it a success." He built his next fundraiser around his passion for film. It was a documentary designed to increase awareness of UBSA among its target audiences; namely students, parents and schools.

By then, UBSA was beginning to get traction. The Atlanta public schools agreed to underwrite the cost of teachers and materials. Today, with more than 200 teachers involved, the program is under way in every Atlanta middle school save one, more than a dozen community centers, and the Service Learning Center at Maynard H. Jackson High School.

UBSA projects are the opposite of make-work volunteerism. Student led, they address serious community issues in hands-on ways that produce significant results. In the recent past, for example, 77 Jackson High School seniors took part in the annual AIDS Walk & 5K Run fund-raiser in Piedmont Park. Askari was among them recording the occasion.

"Students arrived at 6 a.m. and worked until 4 p.m. doing everything from putting up tables, running the route, cheering people on and passing out information," Smith recalls. "They'd spent six weeks prior learning about health and wellness, AIDS and infectious disease. So they were armed with everything they needed before they even set foot on the walk."

As with every UBSA high school outreach, the Jackson students were required to write a 300-word reflective essay describing what they'd learned, how they'd apply what they were taught and how, for example, the community might address the AIDS epidemic over the next 10 years. Only then were they given credit for volunteer service. "If you just tell kids what to do," Smith says, "they never learn what they can do."

• • •

All of which brings us back to Smith's unorthodox parenting, which, as it turns out, is hardly unorthodox at all. "My approach is to support pretty much whatever Askari and Uwezo want to do," she says. "But I won't do it for them. If there's a program, a class, a project, whatever they need, I'm willing to go above and beyond. But they've got to do the work."

Ultimately, she insists, and this is not easy for the overprotective, "When your children are faced with a challenge, you just have to point them in the right direction and let them know they can do it. Too many kids just don't know they can. But believe me they can and they will!"

Chapter

10

Permission

When 16-year-old Juliana first approached her mom with her big idea—transforming her passion for dance into an outreach for young dancers struggling to cover the cost of expensive dancing shoes—Cindy Abel's response was practical and dispassionate. "I asked my daughter, 'There are a ton of nonprofits out there. Why do you have to create a new thing?' Then I realized she'd spent a lot of time thinking about it and wanted to do her own thing. And it struck me, why not?"

With Cindy's permission, Juliana figured out how to solicit and collect nearly new dancing shoes and how to distribute them to other nonprofits around the city. She recruited her two best friends, Meriah and Mekayla, and together they created Pair2Share (see Chapter 6). "They identified places they'd approach, and then they went out and talked to people about what they wanted to do," remembers Cindy, who quickly found herself caught up in the girls' excitement.

The idea gained traction at local dance studios and eventually evolved into Pair2Share, one of the outstanding youth nonprofits supported by GivingPoint. "My daughter found her own passion from what she loved about dance, and it changed her," Cindy says. "Somehow, the act of doing something greater than yourself elevates you."

If Pair2Share epitomizes what energized and selfless young people can accomplish in the world, Cindy's unconditional support represents a vital role parents must play in fanning the spark of a teen's nascent social conscience into the flame of commitment, achievement, personal and societal transformation.

It's easy to over-parent, hoping to promote and protect our children. In fact, we may be unconsciously making them more vulnerable and isolated at a time when technology (e.g., smart phones and all the other social platforms) is silently displacing human contact. Parents must emphasize the importance of societal involvement by giving their children permission to pursue their civic passions. Passion, after all, is the essence of youth. Social commitment not only serves the greater good but also opens up an array of amazing opportunities for a young person's maturation, future success and well-being. They become participants in a benevolent circle

"The act of doing something

elevates

greater than yourself

you."

— Cindy Abel, GivingPoint Parent

of philanthropists, mentors, teachers, sponsors and role models who have rallied to support not only GivingPoint students but also other socially conscious young people.

The irony here is that one might expect parents to shower sons and daughters who make this kind of commitment with praise and support. How great to be blessed with kids determined to ease the loneliness of the elderly, to break the epidemic of teen pregnancy, to improve the lives of children less fortunate, to clean up the Earth's environment or a playground down the street.

Unfortunately, many parents seemingly do not embrace such extraordinary children with the same pride and zeal they devote to offspring who are high school athletes, student government leaders, cheerleaders, math whizzes and honor court members.

Is it lack of awareness, social conditioning or maybe the pressures and "busy-ness" that define and limit our own lives? Remember the old public service campaign, "It's 10 p.m. Do you know where your children are?" For some, it's Saturday noon and just maybe your children are doing something wonderful that you should know about and rejoice in.

Parental support means much more than providing dollars. Some parents cannot (others fail to) support kids struggling to raise the few hundred dollars needed to launch a potentially impactful nonprofit project. True support means caring and sharing, and showing up, posting a positive comment on a social media website, contributing to the GivingPoint blog (or a similar blog), and, to use an athletic image, "making noise" for these wonderful young social entrepreneurs. This is the kind of involvement every child needs and no parent can afford to deny.

It's an involvement that will elevate all of us.

Chapter

11

Parenting

Today's Youth

"Step back from technology's dizzying grip. Be proud to champion a cause, and be humbled to be young once more through the hearts, minds and selfless efforts of your children." —**Derek V. Smith**

I t's increasingly difficult to parent in a technology-driven world. As parents, we face new challenges, many of them unsettling and uncertain. We sense time is being compressed as things happen faster and the decision-making windows grow shorter and shorter. For some, particularly single parents and families where both parents work, parenting is sometimes forced to the sidelines. Relentless technology rushes in to fill the parental vacuum, too often with mindless games or meaningless texts and tweets and other distractions, while we're attending to our otherwise busy lives. Hurriedness causes us to almost unconsciously miss a game, a spelling bee, or the volunteer work our child is doing. We fail to recognize the disappointment in their eyes and relinquish the joy of being a part of their accomplishments. Technological connection via a video screen or smart phone cannot replace vital human interpersonal experience.

Our children watch as our jobs keep us traveling. We're always on the go, chasing a dream, so we can afford the next step on the social ladder. We're doing it all for them—or so we tell ourselves. How else do we save the money to move to a neighborhood where the schools are better? Better schools, better paths for our children, a better future for them. We've made choices and trade-offs that are well-meaning but are often misguided. TVs now have 400 channels, but we rarely find something to watch on television with our kids. We go to bed with a mobile device, and we wake up in the morning to the ping of incoming texts. We're convinced most of it is necessary. Truthfully, we don't know. Instead, we're left with this nagging unsettled feeling.

This is the environment that parents—well-meaning, overworked, doing the best we can, struggling, never satisfied, despairing—contend with. There are no simple solutions. The world has changed, and with it, many of the support systems past generations of parents relied on. We're forced to search for new answers. Not too long ago, the extended family was alive, with grandma, grandpa, aunts and uncles, cousins only a short stroll or phone call away. Doctors and ministers made house calls; they were part of a powerful wireless network that lent a hand or kept us connected to the real world. Today, grandparents—repositories of life experience and loving enforcers of values—are likely to be sitting alone, waiting and wanting to connect and to be included again.

The transfer of values is vastly different in today's technology-driven society. Historically, values were transmitted through tangible personal experiences such as going on Scout trips, attending Sunday school, organizing cake sales, gathering clothing for the needy, cleaning up the beach, and doing blood drives. Place was important to our culture. Today, upward mobility requires lateral flexibility. With rural towns emptying, neighborhoods transforming, families uprooting, schools and houses of worship closing, we're experiencing a death of place and personal interaction, and with it comes a threat to so much of what makes life worth living.

We are becoming an increasingly anonymous society. Our children have electronic "friends." Yet, their circle of personal relationships grows smaller, less intimate and more emotionally detached. Their ability to interpret body language is diminishing rapidly, and that's a real danger. In the shadowy world of the Internet, threats are always veiled.

At the same time, they sense there is something more. Their DNA yearns for more direct human contact and connection (after all, we have been social beings for millennia). For many young people, that yearning leads to unhappy associations with less-than-desirable people and groups. Fortunately, most of our children are seeking meaningful personal connections. They're reaching out to us to help them experience the only

true reality show: the human condition. Yes, it's emotional and sometimes painful to witness, but it is necessary—indeed vital—for their personal growth and empathy for their fellow man.

Young people who have become part of the community of social entrepreneurs give lie to those who predict less than a bright future for this generation. They are truly amazing and inspiring. More importantly, they are fulfilled. As trailblazers and pioneers, they symbolize the marriage of technology and human compassion that will change the world. They carry the spark of transcendence within them. The future will be whatever they choose to make it. With our acknowledgment and love and permission, that spark will become a flame and spread to millions of other adolescents—good kids, unappreciated kids—out there waiting to engage their social passion.

GivingPoint has observed the vital role parents play in this quest. Slow down, parents. Step back from technology's dizzying grip. Be proud to champion a cause. Be humbled to be given a chance to be young once more through the hearts, minds and selfless efforts of our children. As one parent suggests, "Start at home. Do something outside yourself. Your children will take notice. Over time, a synergy develops around the giving back thing. Once you feel it, it becomes a part of who you are, a part of all of us."

This is a critical time, a choice point for parents. Once our children enter college or the job market, the window to instill the seeds of passion for issues greater than themselves begins to rapidly close. Let's reevaluate our priorities and, where appropriate, guide and support our most precious resource—our children—on a path to positively change themselves and their communities through service to others.

Fortunately, most of our children are seeking meaningful personal connections.

Part

IV

The

Educators

Who doesn't recall the teacher, coach or counselor who made a difference at a critical moment in our lives?

The man or woman who took the time, who saw something unique or special in us and laid the foundation upon which our self-image, future success and happiness could be built? As the poet Geoffrey Chaucer phrased it more than 600 years ago, the educator who "gladly would learn and gladly teach."

At a time when children roam the digital highways unsupervised, when both parents in so-called "intact" families often hold full-time jobs and when one in four children under 18 is raised in a household without a father, the importance of skilled, involved and caring educators and mentors cannot be overstated.

Unfortunately, the ranks of these vital individuals—who undoubtedly spend more waking time with our children than we do—are diminishing under the weight of inadequate compensation and budget cuts, tenure rules that value seniority over competency, and the lure of less frustrating and much more lucrative professions. Yet, a cadre remains, marching on undaunted, providing inspiration not only to our children, but also to others. You are about to meet two such individuals.

We call upon you to encourage, recognize and support these immeasurably important people. They are the true guardians of the spark flickering in so many of our children.

Should you want to sample the joy of giving back and to commit to a cause greater than yourself—whether as a parent, mentor or friend—join the educators and prepare yourself for a life-transforming experience.

Chapter 12

Passion

"A child can't learn on an empty spirit."

—Dr. Darian Jones,
Former Principal of The New Schools at Carver

As a child, a special needs teacher, a GivingPoint student mentor and, until recently, a principal at The New Schools at Carver, Dr. Darian Jones witnessed this truth watching too many students arrive at school each morning in "survival mode." These were well-meaning kids, scarred by poverty, abandonment, disappointment and dysfunction, who were expected to perform, against all odds, in the classroom. And they were typically judged wanting if they couldn't. "You can have the world's greatest teacher in the classroom," says Jones, "But you're not learning math."

Jones knows this firsthand. His childhood years were spent in a single-wide trailer in a rural Southern town. He was raised by his father and grandmother. His mother left early, hoping to escape a life where only failure and frustration loomed in the distance. Jones describes his childhood as "North Carolina poor," a far cry from what he encountered in inner-city Atlanta. His extended family was intact and involved in his well-being. His community was engaged, as a street full of neighbors kept a watchful eye on the goings-on of everyone's kids from their porches. Some of his teachers recognized Jones' academic potential despite the joking and endless mischief he seemed unable to avoid. Like his mother, Jones yearned for a life he imagined beyond the place where sky met the tobacco fields. He lived a childhood that was, as civil rights activist Dick Gregory once described, "Not poor, just broke."

Jones was one of the lucky ones. He matured, earned good grades, and became a gifted athlete (he was a star hurdler). After high school, he wound up at Tulane University in Louisiana. After graduating, he took an interim job teaching special needs kids while he prepared to apply to medical school. Something happened: a spark flickered to life. It was his 4th-, 5th-, and 6th-grade students who suffered from cerebral palsy and muscular dystrophy. "They were kids you'd see sitting in a wheelchair at

Darian   **Dr. Jones**   **Jenna**

the mall or hobbling around town with a cane, but kids you never ever had a conversation with," he says.

A man who could leap and hurdle and fly down a cinder track spent a year with students who couldn't walk. Jones had to do everything. The experience changed him forever. "These kids were so powerful," he says. "Some were brilliant. They told me stories I never would have known. They, too, had hopes, dreams and aspirations. Getting to know them, I discovered they had sparks, too. I learned that there is something in all of us that makes us want to get out of whatever wheelchair we're in, be it poverty, abuse, neglect or some other handicap. If you find that thing and free it, it becomes transformative. It's what I wanted to do."

In Atlanta, Principal Jones was determined to prove that empty spirits, like empty stomachs, could be nourished. He realized the next big thing in education was not in the hands of the educational researchers in ivory towers, but in the hearts of the young men and women who streamed into American schools every day. It had to do with the life-affirming human desire to commit oneself to a worthy cause, to be compassionate and caring, and, yes, to be acknowledged for one's contributions.

Jones, whose core belief was to invest young people in learning 24-7, noticed that when his students ventured out of the security of their classrooms to visit nearby Morehouse College (one of the historically black colleges and universities that now make up The Atlanta University Center), "the campus seemed like something from a fairy tale. That's how foreign it was to their world," he says.

He was determined to bridge that gap, which, unfortunately also existed between many young people and their teachers, counselors, parents, authority figures and the world at large. It was a chasm that separated youthful hope and aspiration from the world of possibility. "These kids never laughed," he remembers. "They'd joke with each other and say ugly stuff that was humorous, but as far as a gut laugh at something crazy when you're 14 years old that has tears coming out of your eyes, they never did that."

So Jones began bringing the outside world to them. A former

college track star with a PhD, he had no qualms about marching down the halls dressed as Dr. Seuss' *Cat in the Hat* or Flip Wilson's outsized, sassy Geraldine sporting a wig and stiletto heels. There was meaning to his seeming madness. Jones wanted to build community, a thing too often missing in their world. So he divided classes into Hogwarts-style dormitories, replacing names from the Harry Potter series with outstanding African-Americans.

"Ya'll think I'm cool, but here I am dressed as Geraldine," Jones would tell his gaping students. "But I'm comfortable with that. Nobody is going to change who I am." It was about grabbing their attention and trying to get them to see that it's "okay to be whoever it is you want to be." Jones was also there to get students through the bad parts, "the burdens no 14-year-old should have to carry." The students loved his nonstop cheerleading and shape-shifting. Most importantly, they respected him as a role model.

The gap was bridged. Like some inner-city prophet, Jones had to lead his students to a brighter world where knowledge and accomplishment and achievement were valued and rewarded. He had to instill a mind-set where a college campus or job interview beckoned, rather than threatened. It was about fundamentals such as study, hard work, discipline and self-respect. But the lynchpin that held it all together was what Jones calls "service learning." At GivingPoint, service learning is defined as embracing a cause greater than oneself.

"We discovered," Jones says, "that when you create real service learning—and I'm not talking about community service, which too often means a child cleaning the teachers' room or doing odd jobs—you bring value to a cause or a group of people." Once that bridge was crossed, an ever-growing number of The New Schools at Carver students found themselves eagerly engaged in breast cancer walks, visiting the elderly in retirement homes, working with teen mothers, counseling at-risk elementary school girls, things they cared about personally. Jones and his staff added tutorials that imparted news-you-can-use-style information that The New Schools at Carver students could bring home to their families.

"We'd get everybody to come and sing songs and wear tee-shirts,"

He lived a childhood that was, as civil rights activist Dick Gregory once described, "Not poor, just broke."

Jones recalls, "and walk around the track all night with their teachers to raise money for lupus or whatever the cause. It began to have carry-over value into their academics and self-advocacy, because kids began to realize they could do this. They could apply these same values to their own lives."

Among students thirsting for purpose and meaning, the ripple effect was soon a flood. "Kids began to say, 'Wow, there are people who are equally or more needy than I am. I can do something to fix that!' As they started to embrace these charities and outreaches, they realized, 'I can have power. I can influence somebody else's situation. Maybe there is something to what Dr. Jones is saying about my being able to do the things that determine whether I will be successful in life.' And that really gets them inspired," Jones says.

Around this time, GivingPoint first appeared on Jones' radar. Other school principals hesitated, he says, but he immediately saw the program as a way to connect his burgeoning social entrepreneurs to thousands of their peers all over Atlanta and vice versa. GivingPoint served as a mechanism to promote students' personal passion to impact the world around them and to create their own nonprofits with the help and support of corporations and the community at large.

"I could see the power of it being digital," Jones says. "Students could log stuff and see that other people like them were out there doing good things for other people. They could show that they weren't thinking about themselves but about community and global perspective. For me, GivingPoint became the Facebook of service learning."

For all of The New Schools at Carver graduates, this connection became more intense than any day-to-day interactions with classmates and peers. "Having these real-world experiences, advocating for other people, becoming empowered to help others in a tangible way (e.g., logging hours and writing plans and raising money to donate to a cause you're passionate about), they realized that real people out there care about them and are willing to help them. It is so powerful," Jones says.

So powerful that, under Jones' leadership, The New Schools at Carver produced more Gates Millennium Scholars than all but one school in the nation. If this is a small but honest beginning to an arduous task, it's also an auspicious beginning. In the high-speed world we now inhabit, things happen quickly—and for a reason.

Of course, Jones and other passionate educators are not miracle workers. "Why Johnny Can't Learn" is not a new story, certainly not one confined to our inner cities. Compared with their peers in other developed countries, U.S. students now rank 27th in terms of mathematics, 20th in science and 17th in reading comprehension. Math students in Shanghai outperform their American counterparts by two full grade years. Something is clearly broken. Over the last 50 years, educators have spent hundreds of billions of dollars and churned out every kind of proposed fix—from open classrooms to magnet schools to closed environments where high-maintenance and special needs kids are separated out. GivingPoint is taking a road much less traveled on this great quest, journeying inside the hearts and minds of our youth to ignite the passion that is always there: the intrinsic and powerful human need to learn, to share, to assist the less fortunate; ultimately, to be part of something greater than oneself. Fueling this spark is only a selfless act away.

Chapter

13

Community

"It's one thing to be successful, but it's another thing to be significant and actually leave a legacy behind."

– Michael Cates (1951-2006)

Kevin "Khao" Cates wasn't the first teenager to overlook the wisdom in his father's words. He was moving much too fast, his eye on the prize: fame, fortune, the respect of his peers. No easy thing to accomplish, even tougher for a dreamy African-American kid growing up in Montgomery, Alabama. Too many things were pulling, distracting and tempting, whispering easy answers that could fool him. Khao possessed a rare gift, though. The rhythms and melodies of music swirled and coalesced in his head the way numbers speak to a math prodigy, color and shades speak to a brilliant painter, the seams on a basketball speak to Steph Curry.

Early on, he sensed a higher purpose in this blessing, but what? He was 15 years old and already performing, putting on shows for middle school kids, filling in as a DJ at local radio stations, producing jingles and intros, sneaking into juke joints and after-hours clubs, breathing in the energy he'd build upon and later transform. He glimpsed into the dark side where artists were destroyed by drugs and alcohol and fame. Coltrane, James Brown, Jimi Hendrix, Rick James. He felt its seductive pull. Khao knew the essential loneliness that haunts so many talented young people, worsened by the stain of being poor. Around him, family and friends were struggling with no passion to inspire them or dream to pursue, only the illusion of escape and easy money.

So Khao studied, experimented and innovated, drawing inspiration

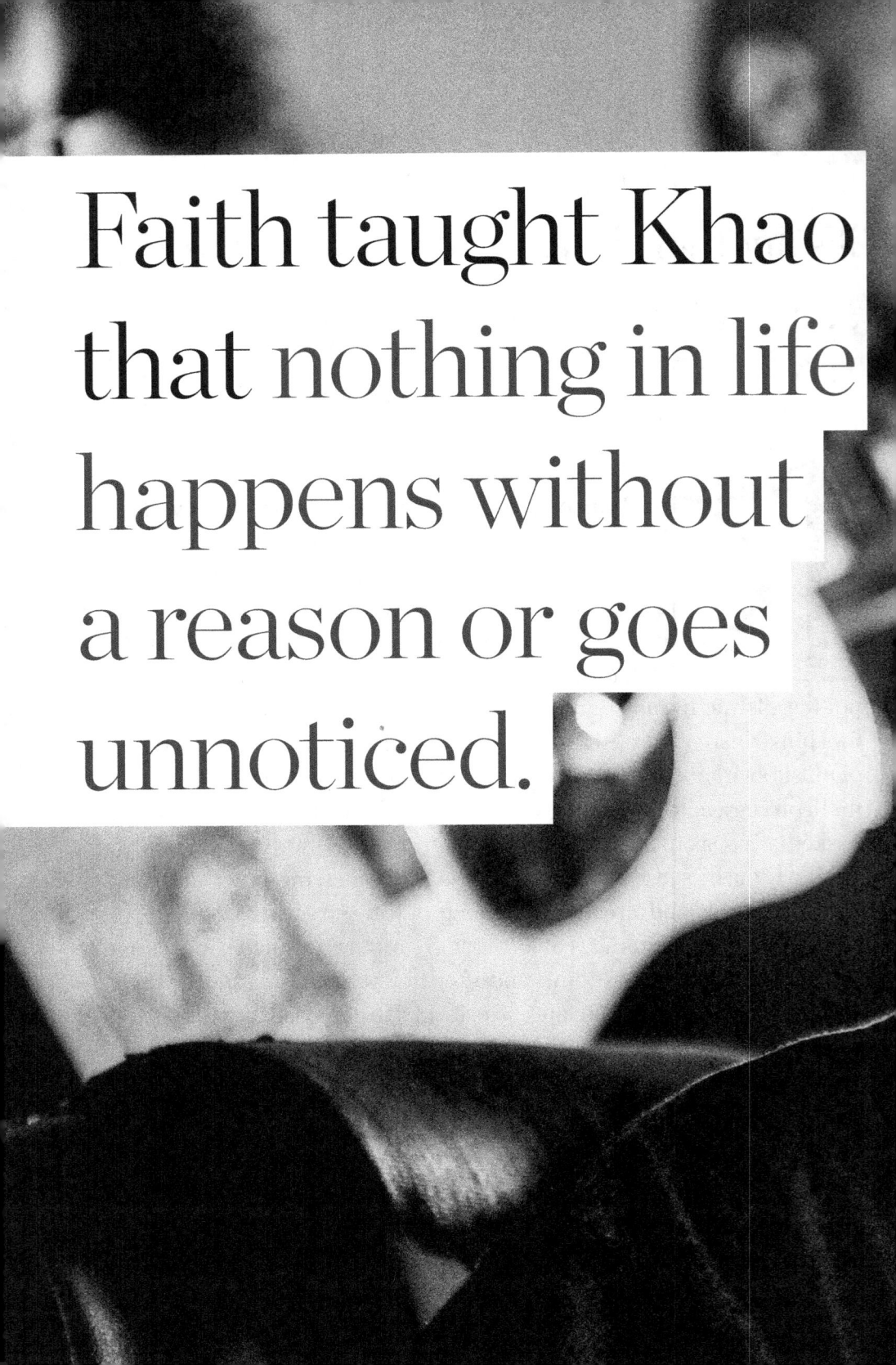

Faith taught Khao that nothing in life happens without a reason or goes unnoticed.

from many sources and streams. When he decided to become a music producer, he took the time to learn the business of music, because he knew it wasn't enough to produce magic, he had to control what he created. Faith taught him that nothing in life happens without a reason or goes unnoticed; experience taught him relationships are vital.

He lent a hand to an up-and-coming artist named Clifford Harris Jr., later known to millions of fans as the rapper, actor and entrepreneur, T.I. Word of Khao's talent slowly spread from Alabama to Atlanta and beyond.

Years passed and nothing happened. Forced to work jobs (a title loan business the best of them) he had no passion for, Khao drifted to the brink of disillusion and despair. Ultimately, an unshakeable belief that he had some higher purpose to fulfill, gave him the strength to pull back. "You could say I've had four strikes," he says, recalling the early years. Scared straight, but still broke, he found himself in Atlanta, living in a car. Along the way, there was a glimmer of hope. He meet a woman, Kimiko Sharpe, who was determined to become a teacher. Now his wife, Kimiko sees in Khao the person he hopes to be, and she describes him as a man with passion; not a talker, but a doer. A man with a big heart who would give his last.

In 2004, the phone rang. "It was T.I.," Khao recalls. "He said, 'Hey you gave everybody else in my crew music; where's my music?' I was like, 'Thought you'd never ask!'" Things began to happen very quickly. Khao's pioneering work on T.I.'s *Urban Legend* album went platinum (1 million copies sold). The following year, he was lead producer on T.I's blockbuster album, *King*. "The world was knowing T.I.," Khao says with a laugh. "He was big. He was doing movies, everything."

Now, Khao's phone never stops ringing. Jay Z, R. Kelly, Lil' Kim, Young Jeezy, Snoop Dogg, Pharell Williams, Ludacris. "All these different artists are seeking me out," he says. "The music business is like high school. If you're the guy who scores the big touchdown, everybody wants to be your friend."

He keeps on scoring. Over the next few years, Khao's records topped more than 30 million in sales. Because he owned his publishing (a rare thing), that guaranteed him royalties and revenue when the hits stopped flowing. Grammy nominations, music industry awards, offers, deals, achievements and accolades poured in. Yet, all the glitz, glamor and success he'd sought left him strangely unfulfilled. "I found myself going to shows like the Grammy Awards and thinking, "This is my sixth time being here. I just wear the same tuxedo, the same everything. I'm sick of this. What's next for me?'"

Once again, fate or destiny – Khao believes it's divine will – provided the spark that sent his life hurtling in a new direction. "I was at my peak in 2007, being honored at another awards show," he says. "Dr. Charles Steele Jr., president of the Southern Christian Leadership Council (SCLC), got up in front of all of us and said, 'On behalf of myself, my generation and Dr. King, I apologize to you all for not passing the torch.'"

Khao sat there stunned. "First, I'd never heard an older person apologize for anything. Second, there was such a disconnect between his generation and mine because they never instilled anything in us. Dr. Steele made me realize that my generation, so busy chasing money, was repeating that same mistake. We weren't reaching out to today's young people. Instead, we were saying, 'These kids are crazy!'"

Afterward, Khao approached Dr. Steele and said, "I want to learn from you and help bridge that gap." In 2008, the two teamed up to launch the Million March 2 Vote campaign in support of Senator Barack Obama's historic presidential run. "Dr. Steele brought the civil rights' community," Khao says. "I brought the hip-hop community. I'm not going to lie, it was a big thing!" So big, President-elect Obama was right there listening when his campaign manager called Khao to express his gratitude. "Here I was starting out as this music guy and now I was out of the box. It gave me this sense of confidence."

He finally understood the wisdom and the challenge in his late father's words. "I didn't know what he meant. But before he passed away, my dad had become a whole different person. All the bad he'd done was made right. Now, all I can think about is how can I be significant?'"

Khao, dedicated husband and father of two young children, wanted a lasting legacy beyond stars and hits. "I knew what I needed to do. I told my wife we were going to get out of the penthouse, that we had to downsize and find a house. I was going to get rid of my truck, consolidate some things. I was going to write a book and save kids. But I had never written a book in my life. I barely read books!"

In 2009, Bridge Da Gap (BDG), Khao's wildly innovative youth outreach comes to him in a dream. "I woke up and I couldn't stop writing," he remembers. Celebrity status forgotten, he's spent the next years writing and composing – fusing technology, hip-hop music, education and life skills into a powerful new platform. None of it came cheap or easy. "I'd been through all these bad things," he says. "So why would the road to significance not have any consequences?"

In a world of constant and unpredictable change, when traditional systems of transmitting cultural and generational values (church, government, school and family) are breaking down, the gap extends far beyond the inner city. "It's a generation gap," Khao says. "No matter what race or color, whether wealthy, poor, or anything else, there's a disconnect between young people, parents and society. Kids are looking for other ways to grow, particularly if they aren't blessed with good role models and mentors. We provide them with the social, educational and emotional tools they need to bridge this gap."

Bridge Da Gap (**http://bridgedagap.org/**) blends music, mentoring and education to inculcate skills that change the lives of socially challenged young people. "BDG instills patience, self-determination, self-love, watching the company you keep, not making excuses in a way that meets students where they are." Khao says. "I produced songs for each chapter. The kids are able to see, able to read along with the audio book, while they're hearing the music."

Self-image, self-esteem, interpersonal skills and relationships are make-or-break challenges in any adolescent's life. Here, too, Khao provides a path forward. "If you're not feeling loved or you've had a breakup with your boyfriend or girlfriend," he says, "you can go to the BDG chapter on self-love and find assurance that you don't need to be a slave of

Self-image, self-esteem, interpersonal skills and relationships are make-or-break challenges in any adolescent's life.

acceptance, that you don't need other people to feel loved."

Like the music industry, the education business is results-oriented. The inevitable question occurs, "What about academic learning and certifiable test scores, the gold standard of education? That challenge has haunted educators for the last half century. Undaunted, Khao set to work again. After endless hours and untold dollars producing and refining, Koolriculum was born. Khao's educational tool kit was state of the art. No old school, raggedy textbooks or worksheets. Instead, gleaming tablets and phone apps leverage the irresistible appeal of music beats and hip-hop rhymes. The power of celebrity teachers like actress Meagan Good engage students in sophisticated, detailed and grade-appropriate content, all created and distributed by Khao's own media company (**http://koolriculum.com**).

BDG is evidence-based. Evaluations conducted by Emory University and behavioral and cognitive assessments undertaken by Pamela Frazier-Anderson, PhD, find solid evidence that the program is effective and well regarded by teachers and students. School boards across the country are incorporating BDG into their curriculums. Its already leapfrogged into schools in the Bahamas. "We're saving lives, stopping suicide, stopping gang wars," Khao says. "I'm watching all this happen. It's better than any award or accolade I could ever achieve musically."

In 2017, Khao is still at it, working out of his comfortable but modest suburban home, building industry and corporate relationships and ever more sophisticated platforms and applications. The next one will engage hard-core and needy students most likely to drop out and continue the cycle of despair and dependency. The spark instilled by Kevin "Khao" Cates's faith and his father is now a beacon illumining the lives of a new generation. Pursuing his passion, his dream is deserving of more than another Grammy.

Part

V

The

Philanthropists

John Wooden is considered one of the finest coaches who ever lived. His UCLA basketball teams won 10 NCAA National Championships over a 12-year period; seven in a row. Continually telling his players and assistant coaches, Wooden is quoted as saying, "Happiness begins where selfishness ends," and "Being a role model is the most powerful form of educating." GivingPoint's young social entrepreneurs need both inspirational and aspirational role models to give energy and light to the spark burning inside them. They also need the generosity and support of caring organizations and individuals. Here GivingPoint has been blessed. Some of the nation's great leaders and philanthropists have rallied behind GivingPoint and its students. They've shared not only their good fortune, but also the wealth of knowledge and experience they've gained along the way.

In the chapters that follow, three extraordinary and impactful individuals recall the people and events that shaped their lives and fueled the spark that still burns passionately within them.

Each philanthropist underscores one paramount lesson: The need to give back, no matter what your station in life.

And the sooner, the better.

Chapter

14

Purpose

"The most important things in life are a kind word, a thoughtful gesture and enthusiasm for what you are doing."

— Ken Langone

As a teenager, Ken Langone dug ditches on road crews building the Long Island Expressway. He served as an altar boy and taught Latin to aspiring altar boys. In grammar school, with a buddy, he delivered half-pint cartons of milk to students whose families were still reeling from the Great Depression and were on welfare. These good works shaped the man he is today. More than a half century later, he recalls his parents, "who had very little," always encouraging him to invite kids "poorer than us, home for dinner." And he still remembers the local church parish publishing a list of who gave what to the Christmas and Easter collections. "My father was always at the lower end of the list," Langone says. "I resented this because in order to give, he went without."

Today, Langone is one of America's leading investors, connecting individuals who put together deals that fund new companies that, in turn, create jobs, drive innovation, and produce wealth. In terms of power and influence, he can pick up the phone and get practically anyone on the line. Personally, he has become immensely rich and intensely committed to helping others. Langone's charitable contributions total in the hundreds of millions of dollars, including more than $200 million to New York University's Langone Medical Center, one of the top teaching hospitals in the United States. And yet, the gruff, straight-talking Langone, a legendary figure on Wall Street, hesitates to call himself a philanthropist. "My father used to say, 'True charity is going without something to help somebody else,'" Langone insists. "I don't go without anything. In fact, there's more to be gained by what you do, than what you give."

Langone knows that no amount of money and influence can deliver the degree of personal fulfillment, satisfaction and human connection that flows when we simply reach out to help others less blessed. As we've seen, GivingPoint students accomplish extraordinary things by embracing causes greater than pure self-interest. Equally important, as Langone points out, this approach moves philanthropy out of the realm of the super-rich and puts it within reach of all of us. "Giving is not just money," Langone says. "Giving is time." And time is a scarce resource for everyone.

For many philanthropists, typically individuals who've spent their lives accumulating the fortunes they are giving away, time is more precious than treasure. "When I spend a whole day at the Medical Center," Langone says, "I could have been working on a deal, reading a book, watching a movie, a million different things that I'll never get to do again because that day is gone."

Yet, Langone does it and is richer for it. "People look at me and comment on my fortune. I'd like to think I'm more than my wallet. We need to broaden the meaning of success so that it doesn't just come from building wealth. Charity is going to somebody who's hurting and saying, 'I know you're going through a rough patch. How can I help?' The most important things in life are a kind word, a thoughtful gesture and enthusiasm for what you are doing," he says.

Such passion elevates the human soul. Good works are within everyone's reach, particularly young people blessed with the invaluable gift of time. "Go to a children's hospital," Langone advises. "Volunteer to sit with one of the kids. Maybe he has a mother who has to work so he's alone. Sit next to his bed and take a Dr. Seuss book or whatever the book for that age and read to him. All the platitudes, all the good words don't mean a thing! You want to help? You have to be willing to help. You've got 15 minutes? Spend it doing something for someone else. Others will follow your example. It's that simple."

The simple blessings of Langone's childhood—the importance of family, the need to give back no matter what your station in life, concern for those less able to care for themselves—and the rigors of the self-made man, make him a keen observer. When he looks at today's young

people, optimism and promise are what he sees, not dysfunction or disappointment. "Young people are focused on social issues," he says, "such as the environment, good health, fitness and service."

From where he stands (the pinnacle of success by any definition), selflessness is not sacrifice. It's a very good investment. "To the extent that you share your good fortune," Langone says, "it gives you a sense of self-worth that gives you more confidence as you attempt to do different things in life, whether it's investing, or a job, or whatever you decide to do. The more you feel good about yourself, the more you're capable of accomplishing. Self-confidence—I'm not talking about arrogance or conceitedness—is a powerful tool in whatever you choose to do."

A lifetime ago, Langone's parents, a plumber and a cafeteria worker, recognized this truth and encouraged it in their son. Today's parents must push past the demands of their own busy lives and careers. They must ignore the insistent messaging of what Langone calls "the world of I and me" and encourage their children to sacrifice and serve. Odd as it sounds, they must give their children permission to ignore the siren song of high school culture and put in perspective the passing glories of athletics and popularity for the lasting glory of good deeds.

Time waits for no one, and it's time for Langone to rush off for another meeting, another deal, another charitable function, this one a benefit for Manhattan's Animal Medical Center, one of his wife Elaine's favorite causes. As he leaves his office on Manhattan's East Side, he laughs and tosses off one of his favorite philanthropic quotes from legendary Texas oil man and wheeler-dealer Clint Murchison Jr.: "Money is like manure. If you keep it in a pile, it stinks. If you spread it around, it grows things!"

Giving is not just money," Langone says. "Giving is time."

Chapter

15

Touching Lives

"Philant touches

It makes you who you are and

hropy
your soul.

gives you a reason to be here."

—Bernie Marcus, Home Depot Co-founder

His is one of the more remarkable modern American success stories. Triumphing over an impoverished childhood in the tenements of Newark, New Jersey, Bernard "Bernie" Marcus went on to cofound The Home Depot, one of the most successful entrepreneurial businesses ever. Yet, if you ask the 86-year-old entrepreneur what makes him most proud now, it's not Home Depot's annual sales of nearly $83 billion, the 365,000 jobs the company generates or his personal wealth.

It's the good work his success allows him to perform. It's the community service that is so much a part of his life and the culture he established at Home Depot. Marcus has a lifelong commitment to causes greater than himself, whether medical research, the well-being of Israel, or his vision of the Georgia Aquarium, to which The Marcus Foundation donated $250 million. "We're in the business of touching people's lives," he says. "Philanthropy makes you who you are. It gives you a reason for being here."

In its purest form, Marcus says philanthropy means giving of yourself. You don't have to be a millionaire to engage in good works. In fact, Marcus knows a number of wealthy individuals who are content to simply write checks because it's the right thing to do, the socially correct thing to do. "They're happy to get rid of the responsibility," he says. "It's like, 'I gave you some money, don't bother me.' "

What's missing, of course, is passion and personal involvement; the commitment to others less well off that becomes a reward in itself. Passion is what drives thousands of Home Depot employees to willingly donate free time to repair the homes of the needy or to maintain the residences of fellow employees who are serving in the military. It's what drives young social entrepreneurs to such extraordinary acts of kindness and compassion—behaviors that will also ensure and enrich their future happiness and success.

Real philanthropy (the love of humankind) is all around us and often under other names: charity, commitment, neighborliness, *tzedakah*

Real philanthropy (the love of humankind) is all around us and often under other names.

(Hebrew for one's obligation to give back to the less fortunate). One of Marcus' early memories is of his immigrant mother leaving their fourth-floor walk-up apartment to carry plates of food to relatives and neighbors who were struggling to feed their own families. He remembers her urging him to skip his favorite charlotte russe (sponge cake and whipped cream sold by street peddlers) to donate a few nickels to plant trees in Israel. "I learned early on," he recalls, "that you have to give back."

Like those trees, the lesson took root. In his 20s, then a hard-charging executive for a California-based home improvement company, Marcus recalls a desperate young manager arriving at his office. The man had just been diagnosed with terminal cancer. "I came to say goodbye," he told Marcus before breaking down in tears. In one of those amazing life-altering coincidences, Marcus had just worked on a fundraiser for the City of Hope, a nationally known cancer research center outside Los Angeles. He picked up the phone and called the president. Sure enough, they were testing an experimental drug. And it worked. The man is alive today. Marcus joined the City of Hope's board of directors and stayed for the next 35 years. "It was my first opening to getting involved in philanthropy," he says. "It set the pace for who I am and what I do today."

Medicine is another Marcus passion. Denied admission to medical school as a young man because of an unwritten quota system that worked against Jews and other minority applicants, he now pursues that passion for the sake of others. At the headquarters of The Marcus Foundation, he reads aloud an unsolicited letter from a woman whose sister received a lifesaving procedure at Grady Hospital's Marcus Stroke and Neuroscience Center, a state-of-the-art acute treatment facility he founded in 2010.

"Your gifts have made such a difference in so many peoples' lives. Everyone (at the facility) was so caring, so passionate about their job."

"This is the name of the game," Marcus says. "When you start early, it becomes a basic part of who you are." Another of his passions is devising unconventional ways to assist disadvantaged youth. (The Marcus Foundation generously supports the GivingPoint Institute, empowering many of the young people in this book.) "If you get kids doing something

Bernie
and Billi
Marcus

they like to do, they are going to do more of it," Marcus insists. "All kids have something that will turn them on. The key is to carry them outside the world they live in." And when we do so, young people and society benefit.

One of his favorite entrepreneurial programs recruited and trained inner-city gang members as teachers' aides, student mentors, after-school program directors and the like. Driven by an unquenchable human virtue—selflessness—these scarred and disillusioned young men were determined that their kid brothers and sisters would have a better chance at life than they'd had. That was the spark. "When you bring them into a world where they are taking care of other people, you're giving them support to take care of themselves," Marcus says. "They brought peace to these areas. Kids were playing outside and it was safe! This gave these guys such pride."

Just experience that feeling once and your life will be changed forever.

This notion of a "cause greater than oneself" underlies this book and GivingPoint itself. "If I was a painter and I painted a great painting," Marcus says, "I'd be proud of it. Philanthropy is no different. You get involved and you help a kid destined for failure. All of a sudden that child, who was going to be drug-addicted or go to jail or be killed, winds up a productive human being. You've saved a life! Tell me how you can replace that feeling!"

Chapter

16

Responsibility

"Because I have been blessed with a talent, I also have been given a responsibility."

—Warrick Dunn, former NFL star

Two days after Warrick Dunn's 18th birthday, his world blew apart. His mother, Betty Smothers, a police officer, was murdered in a botched robbery attempt in Baton Rouge, Louisiana. A single parent, Betty had worked a full-time job and sought out the ability to work overtime at every opportunity available in order to support her six children. She'd dedicated her life to them, instilling by her own example the values they'd need to live full and productive lives. At the time, Dunn, a soft-spoken and determined young man possessed of astounding athletic ability, was looking ahead to college and beyond.

Mother and son had been inseparable, and it fell to young Dunn to identify her body, to face her assailants in a courtroom, to wonder why and what if, and the thousand other torments that accompany inconceivable tragedy. How does one recover from such a devastating blow?

Dunn chose to fill the gaping hole in his life through service. Though still an adolescent, he determined he could best parent his five younger siblings who were reeling with their own grief and loss. Other than his maternal grandmother, there was no one else to step up.

He eventually became his siblings' legal guardian, consciously surrendering the exuberance, freedom, and lack of responsibility so many young people take as a birthright. In the years that followed, he'd forsake the temptations and pleasures of athletic fame, put off marriage and other life commitments until he was certain his siblings' passage into adulthood was secure—the very definition of selflessness. He knew his mom was with

him all the way. "She's proud of the fact that I hadn't gone crazy," he says, "that I haven't gone down the wrong path, that I've done something positive with my life."

Dunn's grief lingered long after his mother's assailants were brought to justice. It was with him at Florida State University where the All-American helped lead the Seminoles to the 1993 NCAA National Championship. It was with him when he was drafted by the Tampa Bay Buccaneers and was named Offensive Rookie of the Year and All Pro three times. He'd spend the latter years of his career with the Atlanta Falcons. At 5 feet, 8 inches, the 180-pound dervish would play an astonishing 12 years in the league and become the 23rd player in NFL history to rush for more than 10,000 career yards.

Fame left him unfulfilled. Betty could never afford the home she wanted so badly, and Dunn's plan to make her dream a reality seemed forever out of reach. But the kindness and compassion that had flowed from mother to son stayed with him, inevitably finding other outlets until it became a healing stream, not only for him but also for others. Wherever he went, Dunn saw other single moms struggling with the same daunting challenges his mother had faced; other children whose dreams were inevitably being ground down by poverty and lack of opportunity. "I knew firsthand what people go through," he says, "and how much a helping hand can mean in a person's life."

In 1997, Dunn created Homes for the Holidays (HFTH), a nonprofit organization that assists single-parent families in achieving first-time home ownership. "I wanted to change lives," he insists, "to impact people for the long term." To that end, HFTH is much more an investment than a magical bonanza. "I want the families to have a sense of personal responsibility," he explains, "and a demonstrated willingness to commit to a new lifestyle. They have to take classes on financial management, on building or rebuilding a credit history, on understanding the intricacies of homeownership."

Now operating under the umbrella of Warrick Dunn Charities, HFTH in partnership with Habitat for Humanity, Aaron's Inc. and other

Dunn's grief lingered long after his mother's assailants were brought to justice.

sponsors, has changed the lives and futures of hundreds of single parents and children. "This is what my mother would be most proud of," Dunn says. "Not my awards, but the way I've used my worldly success to give something back."

In the aftermath of Hurricane Katrina, Dunn's efforts to rally NFL players, owners and fans to assist in the recovery effort generated more than $22 million in contributions. "In Warrick Dunn, American sports may have found its conscience," *The Evening Standard,* a British newspaper proclaimed. Dunn says, "I appreciate the word 'conscience' because that's something that I try to live by and encourage others to follow. Personal values are so essential in steering a life in the right direction."

Another word that defines Dunn is "passion." He seeks out causes he personally cares about. He's there in person every time a family takes possession of a new home. He makes sure there are fresh flowers and groceries, and he oversees every detail right down to laundry detergent and paper towels. "It's the most amazing thing to watch the families receive their homes with such excitement and gratitude," he says. "They're laughing and shouting and clapping and hugging. Of course, I do it for the families. But in some small way, I'm doing it for myself."

Passion drove his involvement with Athletes for Hope, an organization that brings professional athletes, industry leaders and fans together to support charitable causes. "If we do things together, we can touch more people and get more done," he says. Passion drove him to Iraq and Afghanistan to visit American troops. For these and other humanitarian efforts, Dunn was named the NFL's Walter Payton Man of the Year, one of countless other awards he's garnered. Retired in 2009, Dunn is one of the most beloved and respected role models in the game.

"But in the end," he says, "parents are the real role models. They have to control their children and be invested in them. They have to be involved in their lives to make sure they are doing all the right things. They have to shape their minds and teach them to think in certain ways. Parents have that authority, and they need to exercise it."

In college and beyond, years spent driving along Interstate 10 between Tallahassee, Tampa and Baton Rouge, Dunn remained shadowed by grief and loss. Eventually, he sought counseling and decided to confront his demons. In the fall of 2007, he traveled to Louisiana's Angola State Prison to meet face-to-face with Kevan Brumfield, one of the men convicted of Betty Smothers' murder. Dunn was seeking neither confession nor apology—rare things on Death Row. He needed closure. It came, blessedly, when he forgave his mother's killer.

At a meeting with GivingPoint Institute students, Dunn shared these stories and more. He praised the students for their philanthropy and told his story softly, matter-of-factly, but, ultimately, triumphantly. Every kid in the hushed room left determined to dedicate part of his or her life to a cause or need or quest greater than self-interest—exactly what Dunn hoped. Selflessness does not exist in a vacuum. It teaches and transforms by example.

The traits that truly define Dunn are obvious. Not speed and agility, but commitment, compassion, sacrifice, loyalty, generosity, responsibility, not only to family, friends and teammates, but also to those less able to navigate life's turbulent challenges. He has stood in their shoes, tasted the bitter cup of disappointment and despair, and turned it aside to pursue something far greater than himself. In doing so, his pain and loss was transformed into joy and satisfaction more precious and lasting than any fame achieved on the field. His mom is with him, vibrantly alive, guiding him forward. "I know she loves me," Dunn says. "I know that she sacrificed her life for us. I know she's proud."

Proud because Dunn is changing the world for the better. And it all started with a spark ignited by his mom.

Chapter

17

The
GivingPoint
Experience

"Come, my friends,

seek a

wor

'tis not too late to

newer

ld."

— Alfred, Lord Tennyson

We invite you to join GivingPoint or any organization that supports young social entrepreneurs in unleashing the passion and positive energy of youth. With your commitment, we can create an unprecedented level of individual civic engagement, build caring hearts and entrepreneurial minds, and, ultimately, play a part in a second human renaissance—the newer world that Tennyson envisioned and we so desperately need.

Our students are trailblazers. Like pioneers of earlier generations, they need encouragement and support to embark on their unique journeys, to risk the unknown in pursuit of the greater good. At a time when self-esteem is too often confused with self-promotion, they crave neither attention nor treasure. Their illustrious accomplishments have been won through selfless deeds. Now they are poised to become settlers and builders of community, idealists envisioning shining cities on hills.

Such passionate social entrepreneurs are the spark that inspires GivingPoint. In a world often perceived as uncaring and negative, our students are discovering the transformative power of selfless engagement. They are learning this experientially, from peers and mentors and from the shared wisdom of the consummate philanthropists who populate this book. Together, we are witnessing social commitment's positive impact on lives and communities. Like bread cast upon the waters, selflessness delivers a thousand-fold return. All of us are engaged in an adventure to discover what it truly means to give of one's time, talent and treasure.

"You must be the change you wish to see in the world."

—Mahatma Gandhi

GivingPoint wants to inspire you to be part of the change, to nurture the spark within you. Whether it is a flicker or a roaring flame, there is a place and a purpose awaiting you in this new community of social philanthropy. Belong to a group that will welcome you, value you and celebrate with you your unique passions in service to others.

Students: GivingPoint is a complete support system enabling your desire to get involved and give back to those in need. With GivingPoint, you have a partner to help discover your passion or fuel an existing spark for a particular cause; a mentor to help build the entrepreneurial skills, experiences and relationships you need to have a real impact. Through Giving-Point, you become connected to other service-minded youth and become part of an energized community supporting you and your projects. You find yourself recognized and celebrated as you achieve service milestones including:

- Completing verified volunteer service hours
- Participating in online education
- Affiliating with nonprofit organizations
- Raising charitable resources
- Contributing to blogs/sharing photos and videos
- Growing the GivingPoint community
- Building a complete Civic Transcript documenting your passions, service commitment, impact and charitable character to share with colleges and/or potential employers to differentiate you from all others
- Ultimately, experiencing the joy in serving others in need in ways meaningful to you

Parents: GivingPoint is a life-changing platform for both children and family. We begin by asking students to explore this question: What cause or issue are you passionate about that is greater than yourself?

It is a vital question, yet so many of us struggle to formulate or engage. We challenge you to nurture the social passions unique to your children and to give them the opportunity to associate with positive role models. We provide a connection to an extensive network of resources to accelerate your child's learning and service experiences. We welcome you to an environment that reinforces the importance of service and an environment that teaches you how to participate and support your children's (and your children's friends) community service. We invite you to become part of an organization providing pathways to resources that transform youthful passion into robust action. Equally important, we want you to witness and celebrate the personal growth and community impact of young people contributing unselfishly to others.

Educators: GivingPoint is a powerful partner in your efforts to make service learning a vital part of every student's education. GivingPoint provides research and other resources that allow you to put your school on the leading edge of best practices in community service; to give you free access to a state-of-the-art technology platform that can create public or private social media communities to support or fundraise for school and student projects; to provide a verified system of tracking service hours for graduation, the awarding of service cords or other badges of merit using school standards in conjunction with our efficient, fair and visible processes. With GivingPoint, you witness the powerful impact as students showcase their work and motivate others in support of their endeavors. You gain substantial assistance for students competing for scholarships (such as the Gates Millennium Scholars) or awards (such as the Thiel Fellowship's 20 Under 20) and well-deserved recognition. You give administrators, counselors and teachers the ability to understand how their school is impacting the community and enriching the lives of students through promoting service to others.

Nonprofit Organizations: GivingPoint is your technology partner, connecting you to young people with a demonstrated passion for your particular focus. We provide access to invaluable research on the attitudes and behavior of youth volunteers as well as trends influencing their satisfaction and commitment. We reward meritorious service to your organization in a forum visible to parents, friends and like-minded peers. GivingPoint service to your nonprofit appears on youth Civic Transcripts, blogs and picture and video boards. We assist you to better understand your volunteer base by tracking service hours and community contributions, in total or by individuals or groups. We enable you to demonstrate to the broader community of potential supporters your impact on youth and your commitment to developing their service hearts.

We challenge you to nurture the social passions unique to your children

Volunteers/Supporters/Fans: GivingPoint is, in essence, a special group of people who care deeply about youth, each other and creating a legacy of service to the greater good. As a mentor, you assist individuals or groups of students in developing entrepreneurial skills, overcoming challenges and providing needed emotional support. You bring technology, social media, and volunteer experiences to make GivingPoint students better prepared for success in an ever-changing world. You develop educational programs or online modules to impact the skill sets of young entrepreneurs. You provide positive social media feedback by following or cheering on young philanthropists whose work, aspirations or achievements touch you. You introduce GivingPoint to the next generation of service-oriented students, schools, and youth-oriented nonprofits. Ultimately, you witness the truth of the adage, "It is in giving that we receive."

Donors: GivingPoint is an outside-the-box means of engaging in a new philanthropy directly in support of youth. With GivingPoint, you can match your passions with like-minded young individuals who will return exponential value on your contributions. Through GivingPoint, opportunities abound to help inspire a new human renaissance in a technology-driven world. Or simply, to fuel the spark deep within an otherwise unnoticed young person. You provide resources to build next-generation technologies (or to fund a worthy project that is a few dollars short of its goal). You can provide far-reaching educational content for student growth and development or perhaps a personal computer to open the world to a needy student. You can sponsor a GivingPoint Institute student or underwrite a student's transportation to and from a scheduled meeting. You can use a Foundation's resources to reinvent the youth service experience or to invest in a future driven by passionate young social entrepreneurs who need your help to change the world. And, it goes without saying, you will receive a return of infinite value on your investment.

"If you build it, he will come." — Field of Dreams

We've built GivingPoint and have done our best to grow and nurture what we now see as a vitally important undertaking, not only for our youth but also for ourselves. And for the future.

Will you come, my friend, and help build a better world? We need YOU.

To find out more about GivingPoint, to donate to projects, to find volunteer opportunities, to provide support to young social entrepreneurs, or as a nonprofit or school to affiliate with our organization, please visit our website at **www.mygivingpoint.org**.

Follow us on:

Facebook at https://www.facebook.com/mygivingpoint.org

Twitter at https://twitter.com/givingpoint

Instagram at https://instagram.com/givingpoint

Contact us at:

GivingPoint, Inc.

555 Sun Valley Drive

Suite K-4

Roswell, GA 30076

Telephone: 770-709-5010

FAX: 770-709-5016

Email: Administrator@mygivingpoint.org

Social Entrepreneurism:
A Personal
Journey
By Derek V. Smith

"Vision without action is hallucination."

— Dr. Mike Kami

I recall sitting around a campfire on a crisp, clear Georgia night, the sky sparkling like the dome of heaven. A breeze whispered in the pines, sending occasional sparks dancing before my eyes. Some flickered and died; others burned bright and long, spurring soaring flights of fancy. The firelight pushed back the darkness of the surrounding forest, enveloping my friends and me in that familiar sense of security, comfort and companionship that a campfire symbolizes.

In the distance, other campfires twinkled on the mountainside, a sight that recalled summer camp and Scout Jamborees. In my mind's eye, powerful images flickered: Socrates instructing his disciples. Native American elders gathered around a council fire. George Washington huddled with his men at Valley Forge, sparks of determination, self-sacrifice and self-reliance flickering in the night air. It seems a simple metaphor, but sparks have long symbolized genius, insight, greatness and renewal. And campfires are magic circles where we come together to think, teach, share and dream of a brighter future.

I still cannot fully explain what drove us, what signs or signals we read in the campfire's light. Momentous things were unfolding around us, and the campfire drew us into a deep reflection. The world was transforming dramatically. Tectonic shifts were birthing new challenges. Threats and widespread disruptions needed to be acknowledged and addressed. In the last decades of the 20th century, in the vaunted Information Age, the world had become a much riskier place. This was an unexpected insight, given the fact that the Cold War had ended and with it the threat of nuclear annihilation that had hung over the second half of the 20th Century like a toxic cloud. The potential for mass destruction had not faded with the disintegration of the Soviet Empire. The Cold War had blinded us to the ethnic and religious conflicts, economic dislocations, outbreaks, epidemics and crises that are so much a part of today's world.

The ability to unleash terror, panic and destruction—physical, psychological and economic—once the purview of nation states, had shifted to small groups and individuals. These operated beyond the reach of reason, restraint or the threat of mutual assured destruction. Other threats were on the rise. In a digitally interconnected world, anonymity had become a weapon, a far cry from the freedom to reinvent oneself that defined an earlier America when settlers could go west, get a fresh start, and leave no past or footprints.

Like Prometheus's mythic gift of fire, information technology seemed to embody the promise of elevating mankind economically, ethically, morally, even spiritually, freeing us to pursue higher goals and truths. Its avatar, the Internet, was supposed to connect people of goodwill to likeminded individuals in every corner of the planet. We'd bond, befriend and assist one another.

Seemingly overnight, predators, not men of goodwill and noble aspiration, had flooded the digital highways. The communications revolution was delivering risk directly into the workplace and our homes, targeting our children, our aging parents, our access to credit, our good name. On a grander scale, technology's efficiencies and disruptive power were actually widening the gap between the haves and the have-nots, the affluent and the middle and working classes, the technocrat and the employee, the early adapters and those, who for myriad social and historical reasons, arrived late at the proverbial keyboard.

This new technology breached borders and drove wedges between disparate cultures and traditions, inflaming age-old differences and animosities. A odd-sounding phrase jumped the list of my concerns: "asymmetric threat." Risk that seemed to come from everywhere at once, threats posed without a clear-cut adversary, armed forces, leadership or centralized command; risk with no discernible motive; risk enhanced by technology. The asymmetric threat exploded on September 11, 2001, and is increasingly with us today.

Around the campfire that night, these grim new realities ignited a spark that inspired me, Doug Curling and a small group of entrepreneurs to dedicate ourselves, to the extent we were able, to reducing this spiraling risk. We were businessmen and created a new company, ChoicePoint, named for the moment when a critical decision must be made.

Our business model was built around the idea that information technology, particularly the ever-more sophisticated science of data analytics, could be deployed to mitigate the escalating risks facing society. Among financial institutions and insurers—ChoicePoint's primary clients—anonymity and identity theft were enabling new kinds of predatory behavior. Fraud was becoming more sophisticated, large scale, complex and multifaceted. It could penetrate the thickest bank vault and pass like a toxic cloud into our homes.

As leaders of ChoicePoint, we committed ourselves to the highest purpose: protecting society's most vulnerable: women, children, the elderly, the innocent, naïve and unaware. This was our mission. Among the youth and community organizations for whom we did volunteer work, the threat anonymity posed was staggering. Unlike insurance fraud, sexual predation could not be laid off statistically. A background screening tool that blocked 99 out of 100 sexual predators seeking access to a Little League team is unacceptable.

We knew we had to do more. We spent our days developing new strategies, and then we took action. New risk demanded new tactics and tools that could pierce the mask of the criminal while safeguarding the rights of the honest. We sought counsel from wise men and women. Their prescience helped guide us to a transforming conclusion: Information is the most powerful weapon in mitigating risk.

If the world was a riskier place to live, work and do business, we'd use information—responsibly—to offset this risk. Over the next decade, we designed and acquired technologies that could transform mountains of seemingly unconnected data into actionable information and insight that could be used to raise awareness and reduce risk.

Yes, risk also created financial opportunity. Our business model proved powerful. ChoicePoint became one of the largest analytics and data aggregating companies in the world. Our efforts benefited thousands of customers and stakeholders, generating billions of dollars in shareholder value while contributing to the well-being of society.

The value of our services was indeed far-reaching. Our screening tools, donated freely to scores of nonprofit organizations kept hundreds of convicted child molesters from gaining access to children in daycare centers, youth teams, scout troops and other volunteer organizations. We worked closely with John Walsh and the National Center for Missing and Exploited Children. Our technologies were critical in the safe recovery of more than 1,000 missing children. We screened applicants seeking positions in school systems, helping to keep classrooms and the educational workplace safe.

When the Department of Homeland Security set up the Transportation Safety Administration to safeguard the security of the traveling public, ChoicePoint prescreened thousands of candidates. When the Beltway Sniper, John Muhammad, terrorized the East Coast, murdering 10 innocent men and women, our technology helped bring him and his accomplice to justice.

In these years, momentous events unfolded, triumphs and tragedy piled upon each other as if time itself had sped up. We were carried down paths more far-reaching than we'd foreseen as risk continued to grow exponentially. On the other side of the world, men seething with anger and animosity also sat around campfires, planning acts of unspeakable barbarity.

In the fall of 2001, I stood in the ruins of the Twin Towers. Smoke wafted up from the scarred ground, flames smoldered beneath the hissing streams of the fire hoses, headwaters of an endless, nameless river of shattered dreams and vanished lives. I remember former NYPD Police Commissioner Howard Safir standing beside me, grief etching his craggy features.

Around us, ironworkers were wrestling more than a million tons of concrete and twisted steel from the ruins. Police and firefighters were painstakingly probing the debris, still hoping against hope. All of us fell into hushed silence when the remains of a victim were solemnly escorted from the ruins, the silence more powerful than the roar of the jackhammers and the diesel whine of steam shovels.

The success I'd struggled for seemed diminished among the ashes of thousands of my fellow Americans. As a boy, driving into the city with my dad, I remember straining for that first glimpse of the Twin Towers soaring above the skyscrapers of Lower Manhattan, impossibly high, tall and proud in the sunlight. Both now reduced to a gaping hole in the earth. Three September 11 victims—Richard Prunty, Lincoln Quappe, and Brendan McCabe—were from Sayville, my hometown on Long Island, men with families and children, with hopes and plans for the future. Their passing left a tear in the fabric of our community that will take generations to repair.

I was determined that ChoicePoint would do its part in bringing a measure of closure to the families of the victims. Months before, in one of those odd coincidences that seem to mark our lives, Commissioner Safir and a renowned security consultant named Joseph Rosetti, made me aware of the tremendous advances being made in forensic DNA analysis. Cold cases, rapes, murders and other horrific crimes languishing in police files for years were being solved using DNA recovered from crime scenes and matched against the genetic fingerprints of convicted felons. There were thousands of such cases, with traumatized victims living in constant dread and, in many cases, the perpetrators still walking the streets. Here was information that could combat some of society's most terrible risks. Forensic DNA analysis was a new weapon to make the world safer and more secure.

In the spring of 2001, ChoicePoint acquired the Bode Technology Group, a leading forensic DNA laboratory based in Virginia. A decade earlier, Virginia had created the nation's first convicted felon DNA database. Now, Bode technicians using high-speed computers and mindboggling technology that could replicate millions of DNA sequences like copy machines were comparing DNA evidence from thousands of

Their prescience helped guide us to a transforming conclusion: Information is the most powerful weapon in mitigating risk.

rape kits in police evidence lockers and getting numerous hits.

In those exhilarating months, I journeyed to Springfield to celebrate the astounding successes these dedicated young men and women were achieving by bringing justice to criminals and closure to victims and families. DNA's potential was vast. Bode analysts helped solve one of history's great mysteries: DNA taken from bones discovered in a mass grave in Russia were positively identified as the remains of Czar Nicholas II, his wife, Alexandra, and their three children who'd disappeared in 1918. Bode identified Vietnam's Unknown Soldier, Michael Joseph Blassie, and saw his remains returned to his family. There would never be another Unknown Soldier.

Three painful months passed since I stood at Ground Zero. Now, DNA brought me to a dark room, a catalyst that would change my life dramatically. As my eyes strained to adjust to the darkness, overhead fluorescent lights flickered on, bathing me in cold light. I was surrounded by rows of humming freezers, white-enameled units like the ones in a neighborhood supermarket. Each freezer contained hundreds of clear, orange-capped test tubes. Each tube, labeled DM (Disaster Manhattan), contained charred and shattered bits of bone painstakingly recovered by teams of pathologists from the debris of the World Trade Center.

ChoicePoint, through Bode Labs, had been awarded a contract to process DNA from remains recovered from Ground Zero. In the course of this work 1,634 victims would be identified by DNA. Again and again, I observed the reverence with which our technicians treated those tiny fragments. When the DNA they extracted matched a strand of hair clinging to a hairbrush or comb, a blood sample, or some other personal marker traceable to a member of NYC's uniformed services, an honor guard accompanied the remains in silence and dignity back to the city.

My visits to the Bone Room impacted me in ways that took me years to fully understand. The burning embers of the World Trade Center unconsciously sparked a new way of looking at the world and my place in it. Like you, I experienced all the fears and uncertainties that bubbled up in the aftermath of the attacks. I saw young men and women marching off to war. As a person who had embraced every new technology advance, I was stunned that an airliner—a miracle of engineering developed to shrink the world, to build connection, to promote commerce and understanding—could be turned into a weapon.

These men, those victims, that room, those airliners, the thought of so many traumatized and orphaned children growing up without mothers or fathers, haunted me. My own children seemed safe and secure, but really, who could say what the future holds for any of us. I had hit a personal inflection point that sent me in a new direction, speeding thoughts and ideas that had long been simmering inside me.

On the surface, life continued to unfold. For our contributions to the greater good, the U.S Chamber of Commerce named ChoicePoint winner of its Corporate Stewardship Award. Even with success, ironies abounded as predators breached ChoicePoint itself, stealing personal information from our databases. We were early victims in what is now a continuing nightmare for scores of Fortune 500 corporations. It was a very public and very painful lesson, but we learned from it and improved our safeguards dramatically. New York Senator Charles Schumer, once a harsh critic, would later label us the gold standard of corporate data security.

Ultimately ChoicePoint would be acquired by a larger multinational company. As our deal was being negotiated, escalating risk was triggering the near-destruction of the global financial services industry. A few months later—the week Lehman Brothers, a pillar of that world, plunged into bankruptcy—we closed our transaction for cash at an all-time high share price. In a way, it was the bitter fruit of a risky and unsettled world.

When I look back on these years, ChoicePoint's great value was that we helped make society safer through the responsible use of information. We impacted people's lives in a positive way every day—our earlier campfire vision indeed fulfilled. Doug and I, suddenly free of the day-to-day responsibilities of corporate governance, readied for another challenge. The spark that birthed ChoicePoint still burned within us. This spark would take us on another great quest in the not too distant future.

ChoicePoint's sale afforded me a unique opportunity to reflect on my life's journey. "Look to the future with hope and anticipation, but remember and respect the past," my father had regularly counseled. So I started moving forward by looking back and reflecting. I'd always been aware of the clock, as a child and a student athlete, in my career. There was never enough time. Now, I was beginning to understand why. Technology was altering the pace of time. In the short span of my own life, momentous things had unfolded—man's first tentative steps into outer space, the dismantling of the Berlin Wall, the fall of the Soviet Empire, China's ascendancy, the rise of the Internet, globalization, an African-American president.

Changes this overwhelming should have encompassed many lifetimes. But change itself was accelerating. Technology was speeding things up, compressing our lives, shortening the windows we have to make decisions both mundane and momentous. Such velocity was overwhelming and displacing the familiar and traditional, such as how we live, work, parent, transmit culture and values. It was impacting the family, the workplace, the school, the place of worship and bleeding away vital face-to-face human interaction, understanding and empathy.

Exponential change often far exceeds the human ability to keep pace. Exponential technological advance is soul-shaking, the source of the unfocused, but very real anxiety that hangs over so many of us—managers and workers, children and parents, students and teachers, politicians and preachers. We live in history's richest, most powerful and technologically advanced nation, but would our children call this a hopeful time?

They face challenges very different from those of prior generations. My father passed through the fire of the Great Depression and World War II. As a baby boomer, I came of age at a time of inspirational causes and great social movements. By the mid-1960s, the tranquil postwar era was over, but it was, in many ways, still a simpler world, comprehensible to a teenager; an era when duties, obligations and commitments seemed clear as signposts, as regular as the tides. I worked hard, played hard at sports and believed that the future was limitless. I looked forward—as did my friends—to the next good thing.

Today, there is no Great Depression, no unpopular war to protest, no overarching cause or movement to engage the passions of a generation of young people. Instead, runaway technology—texts and tweets, prequels, sequels, CGI and 3D, Instagram, and all the other distractions—is carrying our children off to a kind of meaningless confusion where the commitment, joy and search for meaning that should define youth is often nowhere to be found.

Forty years ago, my hometown resembled communities all across the country, its history and traditions as clearly reflected as the shoppers strolling past the shop windows on Main Street. Yes, there were troubled youths and pockets of need, but overall, as I recall, it was a welcoming place. I was a hopeful kid, blessed with parents whose example early on instilled in me the importance of assisting those in need—an obligation, I've learned, that is its own reward.

Some families went all the way back to the original Dutch and English settlers; others, more recent arrivals, dreamed of fresh air, green space and small-town life. All wanted a better life for their children. The extended family was very much alive with grandparents, aunts, uncles, cousins, living down the street. Strangers were neighbors you hadn't met.

Few were willing to abandon the blessings and demands of small-town life. My mother still lives in the house I grew up in. My father, a passionate man, supported the civil rights movement and committed himself—no popular cause on Long Island—to the struggles of the Native Americans living there. My mother taught school. My earliest memories swirl around both my parents' determination to have a positive impact on young lives and meaningful causes.

It was a familiar place. I knew every kid on my street and they knew me. I had role models. I knew my neighbors, shopkeepers, and the cop on the beat. Today, these face-to-face interactions seem quaint as a windshield wash at the filling station where Bud Van Wyen dispensed gossip with each tank of gas. The family doctor, our minister and my teachers made house calls, all part of a wireless network that linked our community. Parents kept an eye on one another's kids. Values were transmitted in a hundred ways: clambakes and cake sales, clothing drives for the needy, clean-ups on the beach, volunteer firemen, blood drives.

As a kid, I remember zooming down Main Street on my bike, playing football and baseball, and spending summers at the beach. The thwack of the back screen door of my childhood home was as familiar as the ping of today's incoming texts. Place is important. With small towns emptying, neighborhoods transforming, families uprooting (upward mobility often requires lateral mobility), schools and houses of worship closing, we're experiencing a death of place, and with it a threat to all the benefits and blessings of community.

We've become an anonymous society, a nation of strangers. In some areas, 15 percent of the population pulls up stakes each year—a 100 percent turnover every six or seven years. More than a million farming families have left the land, never to return. This exodus does not come without cost. Grandparents, once repositories of life experience and loving enforcers of values, are too often likely to be sitting alone in an elderly care facility.

I can barely keep track of my local community. I don't know the man who fixes the furnace, delivers groceries or installed the bulky satellite dish. It's likely you really don't know the teenager who tutors your child, the athlete dating your daughter, the babysitter who spends hours alone with your toddler. I've made a life a thousand miles from my hometown. My father-in-law's career migrations carried my wife from Pennsylvania to Ohio, Wisconsin, Connecticut and New Jersey.

I confess I wasn't conscious of all these changes, but I sensed the passing of time and pressing things needing to be done. Time rushed forward as it always does. I was in and out of college, then came a loving marriage, parenthood, hard work in the pursuit of a rewarding career, but always sensing the risk levels rising all around me like a flood tide. I decided I had to do more. To raise the siren call, I turned to the power of the pen.

I wrote *Risk Revolution/The Threats Facing America & Technology's Promise for a Safer Tomorrow* to address my concern. One of the warnings sounded was exemplified when Hurricane Katrina devastated New

Orleans. More than 1,800 Americans died and $125 billion in damages were sustained. In Louisiana, authorities had put off strengthening the levees and feeder canals because they'd assessed the likelihood of a storm of Katrina's magnitude was once in a 100 years. That philosophy resulted in tragedy. Decades of inaction had driven the Gulf Coast inevitably ever higher on the risk/crisis curve.

Black Swan events (occurrences that come as a surprise, have major impacts, and are often rationalized after the fact) are happening and with increasing frequency and magnitude. This volatile mix of escalating risk and short-term decision horizons continues all across the globe. The consequences are potentially catastrophic.

Four years later, I authored *A Purpose Under Heaven*, a reader-friendly allegory set in small-town America depicting the threats technology is delivering unnoticed into our homes and communities and the vital role family, commitment and compassion must play in anchoring society. In the words of one book reviewer:

"A small town called New Hope is being turned upside-down by an influx of new people, ideas, and technology. The values that had bound the town together for so long are suddenly challenged. Most of the residents either refuse to believe or simply don't understand the changes creeping in. Some feel the forces at work, but don't know what to do about it; others are taken in by the deceptive faces those forces use."

My reflections ultimately led me to create the Institute of Global Prescience, an interdisciplinary nonprofit research, education and service organization dedicated to the pursuit of prescience (foreknowledge that anticipates global events and trends that are yet unseen). The Institute harnesses the passion of individuals to anticipate issues through sophisticated clue-detection engines that identify potential inflections (in simple terms, departures from a normal or predictable pattern of behavior) in technological, financial and social systems.

The most profound early insight garnered by the Institute is that society's greatest challenge is the widening gap between runaway technology and the human capacity to deal with its often-unpredictable consequences.

"Vision without action is hallucination."

These five words spoken by my mentor, Dr. Mike Kami, convinced me that calling attention to a problem, while important, is not enough to effect transformation. My deepest passion suddenly became clear. I would do my part helping to create "a human renaissance in a technology-driven world." Not by curtailing technology's power or rapid growth, but by harnessing it in service to the greater good, primarily to support future generations in their desire to create a more compassionate and caring world.

• • •

Time passed. Doug and I and our friends found ourselves back around that metaphorical campfire. We focused on the impact of the sweeping changes runaway technology was having on children. We saw a society where family structure too often was breaking down, creating too many isolated, at-risk kids. We felt compelled to act and to create an organization (just like we'd created ChoicePoint in a time of crisis) that would make a difference in the lives of what we were convinced was a generation of young people with unformed futures and endless, untapped possibilities.

We created that organization. We called it GivingPoint and you've seen the early fruits of our efforts in this book through an ever-expanding cohort of young, passionate social entrepreneurs who are stepping up to change our world for the better. We couldn't be more proud.

We invite you to join us.

It's gonna be GREAT!

Acknowledgements

Much like GivingPoint itself, *The Spark: Why Passionate Young Social Entrepreneurs Are Working to Change The World* is a work in progress. At first, I was both astounded and amazed by the passions, hearts and unselfish actions of youth I encountered who were dedicating themselves to issues of social and community well-being. Now, it's become a deep admiration and respect, as I have witnessed so many compassionate, intelligent and capable young social entrepreneurs step forward to engage in causes and issues in which they are deeply passionate. Their stories, too, will yearn to be told. It is my intent to regularly update this book to keep shining a light on the youth, their support networks and the positive impact they have in leading a human renaissance in a technology-driven world. I look forward to including so many of you in the next edition.

Creating GivingPoint and composing *The Spark* has been a remarkable life experience. So many passionate, compassionate and talented people have bonded together and embarked on an exciting journey of discovery and adventure. I am grateful to the following individuals and organizations for their personal and professional encouragement, contributions, critical - yet constructive - evaluations and support.

Doug Curling, my ChoicePoint and GivingPoint partner. Doug has the unique skill of transforming vision into practical reality through operational, financial and interpersonal leadership.

Leah Williamson, my executive assistant and extraordinary person. Leah makes my world hold together through skill, dedication and a little magic. Our family is blessed that she is such an integral part of our daily lives.

The GivingPoint team and Board of Directors. Their passion and unparalleled commitment to our young social entrepreneurs is remarkable and inspiring.

Vince Coppola, my co-author and friend. Our writing adventures have taken us through the changing risk structures in society (*Risk Revolution*) to how technology is impacting our communities, spirituality and family values (*A Purpose Under Heaven*) and how why young men and women are working to change their world in meaningful and purposeful ways (*The Spark: Why Passionate Young Social Entrepreneurs Are Working To Change The World*). Vince's ability to turn personal experiences of diverse people into engaging and meaningful stories is a rare gift of empathy, skill and perspective.

Matt Strelecki, this book's art director. Bringing together a concept and manuscript, Matt has delivered an organized and expertly presented book in an engaging and easily readable presentation.

The Marcus, **Zeist** and **Myfifident Foundations** and **New Kent Capital**. Their belief and financial support of the power of social entrepreneurialism have rallied our youth to transform the communities in which they live.

The professionals and their firms who have become instructors, presenters and mentors for our GivingPoint Institute students. What an impact they have made!

My wife **Lisa**, daughter **Hanley** and son **Tanner**. For unwavering support of my many journeys, seemingly crazy ideas, ventures and adventures, you are the never-ending source of energy, joy, inspiration and love that is the true spark of my life.